I Teach

A GUIDE TO INSPIRING CLASSROOM LEADERSHIP

Joan Dalton and Julie Boyd

Heinemann
Portsmouth, NH

HEINEMANN EDUCATIONAL BOOKS, INC.
361 Hanover Street, Portsmouth, NH 03801
Offices and agents throughout the world

ISBN 0-435-08782-7

Published simultaneously in the United States
in 1992 by Heinemann
and in Australia by
Eleanor Curtain Publishing
906 Malvern Road
Armadale 3143

Production by Sylvana Scannapiego,
Island Graphics
Edited by Ruth Siems
Text design by Antoinette Monteleone
Cover design by David Constable
Typeset in 10/12 Helvetica light by Optima Typesetting and
    Graphic Design, Melbourne
Printed in Australia by Australian Print Group

*This book is dedicated to teachers
everywhere who are committed to
their own growth, and who are working
to make a real difference to the world
through the way they teach.*

▼ CONTENTS ▼

▼ ▼ ▼ ▼ ▼ ▼ *About teaching and leadership*

No printed word nor spoken plea
can teach young minds what they can be.
Nor all the books on all the shelves,
But what the teachers are themselves.

Teaching: a significant profession

This book is for teachers everywhere who are striving to make a difference to the lives of the learners they teach. It is for teachers who are as committed to their own learning as that of their students. And it is for teachers who have the vision and the courage to be part of an increasingly complex and demanding profession, where change is a constant in their day-to-day teaching lives.

Such teachers understand the importance of finding ways of preparing learners to thrive in a world characterized by rapid and accelerating change and complexity, an amazing explosion of information and choices, and an urgent need for people and nations to co-operate and work together. They know that the way to do this is by focusing on human growth and development, by building lifelong attitudes to learning, and by empowering learners to become what they can be — self-aware, reflective thinkers who know how to learn, who have a strong sense of self-worth and inner direction, who can take responsibility for themselves, and who have a sense of responsibility toward others. This what empowering learners for the future is all about.

We work with many such teachers across Australia and further afield. They have helped us to learn many things, and to make some powerful connections in our own thinking and learning. One such connection we've made is that

teachers are leaders.

Our experience in educational administration, our understanding of the literature on leadership, our work with business and industry, and our observations of many, many wonderful teachers in their classrooms have led us to what we think is a significant conclusion. And it's worth saying again — as teachers, we are leaders.

The same qualities, principles and skills of leadership that many teachers are using, and have used in their classrooms for a long time, are the same qualities, principles and skills increasingly sought by business, industry and the broader community. What they know as 'empowering leadership' is what we know as excellent learning and teaching practice!

What business and industry are learning is something that good teachers have always known — that *people* are the key to success, and that this is achieved through a focus on human learning and development.

We as teachers need to learn and acknowledge that we are leaders, and we need to start seeing ourselves as such. The very essence of professionalism in education pivots around this concept, and it is certainly a fundamental premise of this book.

This book is not only *for* teachers, it is *about* teachers, most of them real teachers we have worked with. These teachers seem able to demonstrate a way of leading that inspires success and a love of learning in students that will last them all their lives.

We have spent a long time teasing out, and often struggling to pinpoint, how it is that they are able to do this. In so doing, we think we have made another significant connection. It seems to us that great teachers know, either consciously or intuitively, that true learning occurs only when people take control from within and, as classroom leaders, they teach from within. They share their internal power in ways that help learners to take increasing control over themselves. This means that they carry inside their hearts and their heads, as part of their deep inner core, an enduring set of principles by which they teach and lead.

These teachers are making a significant choice. Instead of choosing to feel overwhelmed by the knowledge explosion, the pressure of external forces and 'more and more to teach', they are choosing to move to an economy of learning — learning and teaching that is more economical because it is centred on principles that underpin the way they operate as teaching professionals. Unlike packaged programs, models and activity books, such principles offer guidelines against which to measure the worth of external resources. They provide a holistic or 'big' picture for us all to work towards in terms of leadership, learning and human growth, relationship with self and others, individuality, interdependence and harmony.

These principles form the basis of this book. Each section is interdependent; some principles fit easily into one section whilst others could encompass several. We have tried to group them in a way that will stimulate you to reflect on your own teaching and learning, for this is the heart of the book — the 'inner you', your own reflections and learnings.

Reading I TEACH

When we began this book, we had clear purposes in mind. We wanted to affirm the outstanding work that teachers do every day of their classroom lives — to nurture it, to support teachers, and to share what we're learning from them. We wanted to acknowledge teachers as leaders, and introduce the notion of principle-centred teaching. And we wanted to show what these principles look like in practice.

We have tried to model what we think is important to the future, and to good learning and teaching practice. We know that our brains seek to make meaningful connections and that stories are a powerful aid — hence our strong focus on vignettes or short stories. We acknowledge that people learn in different ways by using photographs, diagrams, charts, story-vignettes, narratives, quotes, and journal reflections. We understand the importance of relevance and context, and have drawn our examples from real teachers, wherever appropriate and possible. We have identified the key principles, and have drawn the pieces into a whole or 'big picture' in a way that offers opportunities for reflection, for affirmation, for self-evaluation, and for growth. And just as good teachers do, we have tried to share something of ourselves — our beliefs and our vision for what teaching can be.

This is not a book about curriculum — it is a book about people, about learning and human development. This is not a book of answers or 'activities' — it is a book that raises key principles, concepts and issues. The 'On Reflection' section suggests different ways to use this book, but we hope that you will also create your own. Its purpose is to encourage you to look within yourself, to question, to share your thinking and to stimulate you to explore further. Its challenge is for you to transfer these principles to your own teaching.

We hope that by reading *I Teach* and reflecting on its messages, you will not only find affirmation for what you are already doing but will discover more about yourself and the principles that are essential to inspiring classroom leadership. For it is only when we become truly self-aware that we can choose principles and purposes to teach and live by.

And once we make that choice, we can acknowledge ourselves as teachers, as leaders, as members of a significant profession. It is then, when people ask us what we do, we can proudly and openly say,

'I teach.'

▼ Empowerment
▼ in
▼ action

The future is not some place we are going to,
but one we are creating.
The paths to it are made, not found,
and the activity of making them changes
both the maker and the destination.

— *Commission for the Future, 1989*

As classroom leaders, we need, not only an understanding of the centrality of empowerment to the future, but a clear picture of the learning and teaching principles which are significant in helping students to become meta-learners and thinkers, which build responsibility for, and commitment to, learning, and which help learners to work with others in mutually co-operative ways.

The 'Campbelltown story' provides one example of what can happen when these principles are applied in context. As such, it is a story worth telling. In its telling, we have highlighted the students' achievements, and have chosen to use vignettes as a way of providing insights into how their learning, and their project 'Overflow with Info,' developed.

We have tried to remain true to the 'realness' and the spirit of the 'Campbelltown story', including at the same time some of the 'gems' teacher Glenn Bromfield shared with us. And being teachers ourselves, we have certainly tried to include the 'pieces' that we think model important learning principles and demonstrate empowerment in action.

The Campbelltown story — a brief picture

'We've figured out the cost of our 'sleepover' — and adding together the hamburgers, fish and chips, and the videos to watch when we've finished, it comes to $17.50,' said Michael.

'The school will be happy to cover that cost,' smiled Roger Edmunds, who was the principal of Campbelltown District High School. For this was no ordinary sleepover.

Michael was one of four Year 9/10 students, who with their information technology teacher Glenn Bromfield, had planned a mid-week sleepover as an efficient way of setting up their school's new computer network system from Years 1 to 10.

It was the installation of this computer network system, and the ensuing need to train all students and staff, combined with the availability of some government funds to encourage student enterprise and decision-making, that led to the development of a significant learning project for Glenn's Year 9/10 computer class.

The initial project goal was to teach other people the information technology skills they themselves had acquired. What followed went way beyond what Glenn had ever dreamed of and demonstrates what a so-called group of regular students can achieve when they learn to take increasing control of their learning and to work together as a team.

Student achievements

• In pairs, the class tutored students and teachers across the school;

• As a group, they completed their Year 9 & 10 information technology syllabus by mid-year, and advanced into the Year 11 and 12 syllabus;

• Students negotiated with the local adult education office, organized and ran a computer course for parents and community members;

• Students organized and staged a statewide expo of technology, 'Technofest', seeking and gaining wide support and sponsorship from business, industry and community across Tasmania;

• Concern about the need to encourage more girls into the field of technology led one group to organize a 'Girls in Technology' conference, which brought together teams of students and teachers from schools across Tasmania;

• Awareness of the need to share information and to celebrate success led students to present workshops and papers at a number of educational conferences, including the fifth world conference on 'Computers in Education'.

INTRODUCTION TO COMPUTER TECHNOLOGY

A five week course to be conducted by the "Overflow with Info" student enterprise group

Commencing on Wednesday, September 14 (7-9 pm) at the Campbelltown District High School Library

Fee: $20 payable to Adult Education before September 9.

Topics covered (In an informal manner) will be:

Introduction to computers and the use of network systems

Introduction to data bases and collection of information

An experience in computer programming

The future of information technology

Basic word processing techniques

Enrolment:

Contact Jenny Upton or John Watson at the Adult Education office,
The Grange,
Campbelltown. Telephone: 811283

Enrol early:

Maximum number of enrolments will be 22

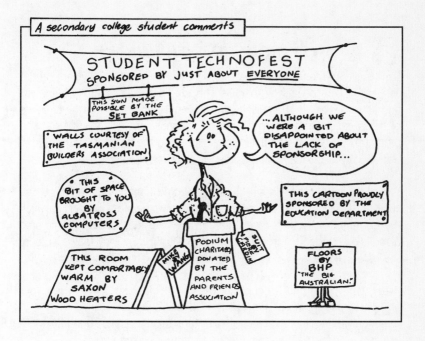

How did these students manage to achieve so much? Certainly, the notion of students and teacher installing a computer system together on a Wednesday evening says something about the school climate and the belief that ownership and commitment to learning are built when students contribute and share responsibility within a school. But there's more to the story than existing school climate, and over the following pages the story unfolds further . . .

▼ *INTRODUCING THE IDEA* ▼

'This is perfect for what we want to do with our computer system, and it just might provide a way to meet the staff's professional development priorities this year.' Warren Pill, deputy principal, had just shared the contents of an Education Department letter inviting submissions for student enterprise projects with Glenn Bromfield. They discussed the computer expertise of Glenn's Year 9/10 class, and agreed to take the idea to them.

The next day, Warren, Roger the principal, and Annette Salter, Year 9 and 10 English teacher, were invited to be part of a whole class meeting at which the contents of the letter were shared and the idea raised. After some discussion, students agreed to think about it further. They took a copy of the letter and agreed to bring their thoughts to Thursday's class . . .

'Now that you've had a couple of days to think about it, what are your thoughts about going ahead?' asked Glenn.
'I reckon we ought to give it a go,' said Rachael. 'It could be good fun.' This was accompanied by vigorous nods from around the room.
'Okay, then,' said Glenn, 'we shared one idea with you—that of teaching the staff computer skills—let's brainstorm, and see what else we can come up with.'
'We could teach the kids as well as the staff,' Kelly offered.
'We could run a technology night like the one you organized last year,' suggested Michelle.
'What about teaching the elderly people in the Home over the road?' asked Paul.
'I reckon we should teach our parents,' said Enzo.
'And I reckon we should find a way to encourage girls,' added Sonia.
Glenn wrote all suggestions on the whiteboard and the list grew. Finally, as ideas petered out, he said, 'We've got a whole list of ideas here. How are we going to arrange them in order of priority?'
'I think it's going to depend on what we can manage,' said Kelly looking thoughtful.
'Yeah, but it should be stuff we really want to do,' commented Tim.

Building from these two comments, Glenn negotiated two clear criteria with the class — one, that it should be manageable in terms of time, human and physical resources, and the other, that it should be enjoyable and involve things they really wanted to pursue.

They then applied the criteria to establish priorities and goals, and agreed as a whole group on the activities they would run to achieve their goals.

As the session drew to a close, Tim raised the question: 'How are we actually going to run all this?' to which Glenn's response was, 'I'd like this to be your project, not mine. I'll help you in whatever way I can and I know the other teachers will, too. What's the next thing you think we need to do?'
'We need to get organized,' said Rachael.
'Well,' said Glenn, 'maybe Mr Pill could talk to you about different possibilities for organizing yourselves because he's really good at that sort of thing . . .'

Classroom leaders:
▼ Provide real think-time
▼ Promote engagement in authentic, purposeful learning
▼ Offer open-ended learning opportunities
▼ Understand that learning needs to be enjoyable

▼ *SETTING UP* ▼

'How are you going to set yourselves up to manage the whole process?'
One suggestion from the class in response to Warren Pill's question came
from Vanessa. 'We could run it like a club and elect a president and a
secretary, and so on.'

'That's one way,' replied Warren as he wrote up the suggestion. 'Let's look
at some others as well,' and he outlined a couple of different models on
the whiteboard. Students added some more ideas. Glenn then made his
agenda clear: 'Whichever way we choose, I'd like to see us come up with
something that enables everyone to contribute, and I'd also like to see you
all have a go at different roles because it will give you broader experience
and you'll gain new skills. I believe that it's important to appreciate what
other people do and other people's skills — it's easier to do that if you have
had a go at it yourself.'

Discussion around Glenn's perspective resulted in general class agreement
in terms of being able to use their strengths and interests, as well as learning
to take on new roles or jobs. Students also suggested that the model chosen
should be an efficient way of operating.

The class then looked at the advantages and disadvantages of each model,
and agreed fairly quickly that the best way of operating would be to work
in small teams, with responsibilities evenly distributed.

They brainstormed all the jobs that would need to be done. The information
on the whiteboards was growing all over the place at a rapid rate and Warren
suggested, 'How about we make a visual map or plan to help us organize
all this information so that we can see it more clearly . . . And remember
— its just like working with Lego blocks — we can pull pieces apart and
put them together in different ways, so if it doesn't look right and we need
to change things, we can.'

Warren and Glenn, acting as scribes, created a large diagram on the board,
changing and modifying according to student input:

'No, that's not right — rub it out.'

'That's not what we mean.'

'If we do it that way, does that mean . . .'

'That's beginning to look like a co-ordinating group. If we have one, we're not going to stick the same people in it are we? I'd like to move around.'

What finally emerged were four major groups, each with a distinct set of responsibilities. There was to be a *Budget and activities group* which was responsible for handling the group's money and budget, and keeping financial records up to date. The *Promotions group* was to handle all the advertising and publicity, and to be responsible for keeping the school and community aware of what was happening. The *Evaluation group* was to evaluate not only the progress of the actual project, but also the existing computer knowledge of the people they were going to teach and the progress they made in learning. A small *Central co-ordinating group* was to take responsibility for overall co-ordination, but all decisions were to be brought to whole class meetings, which, it was agreed, would be held regularly for planning, reporting back and evaluation purposes.

'My head feels a bit like a waterfall at the moment — it's overflowing with info . . .!' quipped Tim. Everyone laughed, and the name of the project, 'Overflow with Info', was born.

Over the next month, each group worked hard to prepare information for an overall submission to the Education Department. Careful planning, continual adjusting of goals and checking against criteria, networking effectively and use of community resources resulted in the development of a professional, detailed submission, and the awarding of $1000 to put their plans into action.

Classroom leaders:
▼ Build from what learners know and can do
▼ Explain the purpose
▼ Make use of visual organizers
▼ Encourage thinking in metaphor

▼ *TALKING WITH WAYNE* ▼

As the bell rang for recess, Wayne approached Glenn.
'Mr Bromfield, can I speak to you for a minute?'
'Of course, Wayne. What's up?'
'I really want to be involved in the budget group because it's something I'm good at, but I don't want to have to do any speaking in public. One of the reasons I want to become an accountant is because I won't have to deal with people too much.'

Glenn responded 'I can certainly understand how you feel about speaking in public — it's something that most of us find really hard. It doesn't matter what job you take on these days, you still have to deal with people, accountants included! What is important is to be able to share our ideas, and I know that you have lots of good ones. I've noticed sometimes you seem to have something you want to say and you hold yourself back. That must be frustrating for you.'

Wayne nodded, and Glenn went on to ask 'What would need to happen in class for you to feel comfortable about sharing your ideas?' Wayne replied that he would want people to listen to him and take his ideas seriously.

Glenn reminded him, 'When the group met last Saturday night to develop a draft of our standard operating procedures, you might remember one of the things we talked about was the need to develop some ground rules for how we treat each other in meetings. It's on the agenda for our next whole group meeting. We can build these ideas in, too.'

Glenn continued, 'If we were able to make sure this could happen, what would be something that you might like to work towards being able to do — maybe as a personal goal for yourself?'
'Well,' said Wayne, 'the budget group gives a regular report at meetings. One day I might be able to be their reporting rep . . .'

Over several weeks, Wayne gained confidence to speak up in general, and fulfilled his goal of reporting back on behalf of his group. Eight months later, he volunteered for, and was successful as, master of ceremonies in front of one hundred people who were gathered together for a state student enterprise conference.

Classroom leaders:
▼ Take time to support individuals
▼ Give feedback on observations
▼ Help realistic goal-setting

▼ *LEARNING ABOUT LEARNING* ▼

'How do we assess how things are going?'
'What does evaluation mean?'
'How can it be useful?'
'What do we do this for?'

These were the sorts of questions Annette Salter was confronted with when she was invited to act as adviser by the evaluation group. She tackled this in a way that helped the group to clarify for themselves the purposes of assessment and evaluation. From this point, they looked at a range of techniques or methods, worked out the most appropriate ways to identify the current knowledge and skills of the people they were going to be teaching, and decided how best to monitor the progress of the project. Video was to become a major tool for giving the class feedback on how they were working as project developers, and they decided to develop a staff survey as the best way to get information quickly about both staff and students they would be teaching.

Annette helped them to look at different kinds of questionnaires, and to focus on asking key, open-ended questions in order to reduce their very long lists of questions to a more manageable few.

'How are you actually going to get the staff to do this?' Annette asked.
'Can we take it to the next staff meeting?' Andrew suggested.
'I'm sure that could be organized — it's a good idea,' agreed Annette, 'because it's the only time the staff are really all together.'
'Well, perhaps we could explain it to the staff,' volunteered Vanessa, 'and give them a couple of days to fill it in. If we give them any longer they might forget.'

'And we'll tell them that we'll come around and collect them individually,' added Fiona.

'Sounds good,' said Annette. 'So — who's going to take it to the staff meeting?' Six pairs of eyes looked momentarily at each other, and they chorused, 'We all are.' And they did!

Classroom leaders:
▼ Encourage learners to ask their own questions and seek their own answers
▼ Share their power with others
▼ Use a variety of strategies

▼ *TEACHING SNOWBALLS* ▼

'. . . and so to summarize our report,' said Tim, 'we've got all the information back, and a good idea of where staff and kids are at. We'll have all that information organized for you before people start working with their particular classes. What our group would like is some help in figuring out how we're all going to teach them.'

Sonia, whose turn it was to chair the meeting, looked at Glenn and asked, 'Mr Bromfield, would you help us with this one because we've only got a week before our tutoring sessions start.'

Glenn looked very pleased. He'd been feeling a bit worried because, although there was a place on the agenda for 'Adviser's comments', he hadn't been given a specific job to do for a couple of weeks!

'There are different ways we could look at it,' he said 'One way is to think about what actually helps people learn.' By getting the group to connect learning to their own personal experiences, he drew out from them, and listed on the board, a range of learning and teaching strategies. They discussed the appropriateness of different strategies for different situations, and Glenn made the point that people learn in different ways and that sometimes a range of strategies needs to be tried.

As a group, students decided that they would indeed like to try all of them, and agreed to include regular feedback sessions on their meeting agenda, so that they could talk about what worked, what didn't, with what age groups and in what situations.

One of the first teaching issues they decided to address was how to help other students learn to take care of expensive computer equipment. Glenn modelled one way by asking them to physically imagine, 'If you were a computer, how would you like people to treat you?' There was much laughter at some of the 'tongue-in-cheek' responses to this, but subsequent comments showed that the students appreciated the use of fantasy and imagination as a very powerful learning tool.

One strategy tried was the 'snowball technique', where two students in a class — a girl and a boy, at the request of the 'girls in technology' advocates — were taught a new skill by their Year 9/10 peer tutors. They would then separate, and teach two other classmates, and so it would spread out, 'snowballing' until all the students in that class had been reached.

In the first whole-group feedback session, each tutor-pair shared their teaching stories, others asked them questions and offered constructive suggestions. Kelly and Enzo, who'd been tutoring Year 4, shared their experiences with the 'snowball technique'. Questions from the group included 'How many days did it take before you were sure that all the kids could do it?' and 'What would happen if one kid didn't "get it" and taught the others wrongly?' Students concluded from their discussion that this technique had been successful because the skills that Enzo and Kelly had been teaching were very specific, but that it might not be so successful in other situations.

Students continued to make mature and fascinating observations during their regular feedback sessions. Over the months that they tutored, they concluded that the 'whole class' model was the least effective, commenting that 'it wasn't much of a way to teach', that 'we found kids were not paying attention' and that 'when we tested them, not everybody had picked up the skills.'

They found small groups to be the most satisfying for everybody, commenting that 'everybody got a go', 'they all had the chance to talk and ask questions', and 'they really helped each other learn the skills well.'

Classroom leaders:
▼ Foster learning with and from peers
▼ Develop understandings of many ways of learning
▼ Appreciate the importance of imagination in learning
▼ Help learners to use the metacognitive cycle of plan-monitor-evaluate
▼ Help learners to develop context appropriate strategies

▼ *MAKING MISTAKES* ▼

'Rachael, there's a guy on the phone from Channel 2 wanting to talk to you about the *7.30 Report*. Do you know anything about this?' asked Glenn.
'I think so,' said Rachael.
'Well, you'd better take the call because he's waiting — and then you'd better come straight back to me and tell me what it's all about.'
Ten minutes later, Rachael returned looking very excited. 'They're coming!' she exclaimed.
'Perhaps you'd like to explain what's going on,' suggested Glenn, looking puzzled.
'I wrote a letter to the *7.30 Report* telling them that we're having a 'Technofest' and they're coming to film us.'
'Who knows about this?' asked Glenn.
'I wrote it on behalf of the promotions group,' answered Rachael, 'but I haven't told them yet.'
'So you didn't discuss it with your group. I wonder whether you talked with a teacher. Remember, one of our basic class agreements is that an adviser must co-sign any letters that leave the school . . . did you get a teacher's signature?'
'No.' And Rachael's face began to lose its glow.
Glenn continued, 'So I didn't know, none of the other advisers knew, your group doesn't know — does the principal know?'
'No.'
'So what are you going to do about it?'
'I guess I've really stuffed up. I suppose I'll have to tell Mr Edmunds, and I'll need to talk about it with my group — I'll have to do it quickly though, because they're planning to come on Wednesday.'

'Rachael, do you understand why we had those procedures in place, and how when they're not followed it can make life difficult for other people?'
'You mean like when the budget group mucked up their books because they didn't follow the procedures they'd set up — and we all had to put things on hold for a week till the auditor came in and helped them get sorted out?'
'Yes,' nodded Glenn. 'Sometimes when we think we're doing the right thing we can inadvertently create lots of difficulties for everybody else. That's why we talked about those procedures in the first place.'

Rachael looked downcast. 'Yeah, I realize I've done the wrong thing . . .'
Glenn asked, 'Can you remember back to when we first started our project,
we talked about 'having a go' and how that might mean things going wrong
sometimes?'
'Yes.'
'Can you remember what we said we'd need to think about?' Glenn probed
quietly.
'Yeah,' nodded Rachael, 'if things go wrong, to pinpoint what happened, fix
it up, and make sure it doesn't happen again. So . . . I've made a mess of
things and I need to try and fix it up — but can I ask you to help me?'
'Yes, you have done the wrong thing,' agreed Glenn, 'but I'm pleased that
you've acknowledged that. I'm quite happy to help you try to sort things out.
It seems to me that you're clear about the first steps you need to take. You've
really set quite an exciting challenge for yourself, haven't you?'

Classroom leaders:
▼ Understand the importance of risk-taking in learning
▼ Focus on learner self-evaluation
▼ Develop learner responsibility to self and others
▼ Reframe mistake-making

▼ *MAKING CHOICES* ▼

'What's up, Kelly? You're looking a bit agitated.' Glenn remarked quietly, as they walked along the corridor together.
'I'm feeling really fed up — Sonia's being a real pain.'
'Would you like to talk about it? I've got a few minutes before my next class.'
Kelly nodded. 'I need to do something but I don't want to lose my temper.'
Finding a quiet space to sit, Glenn helped Kelly clarify what the issue really was. It seemed that Sonia and Kelly were having some major disagreements about the way things should be done in the co-ordinating group. Kelly's concern was how to disagree without them 'attacking' each other.

'One way to think about it,' Glenn suggested, 'is to realize that we have choices in how we deal with conflict. We can choose to act in a way that will resolve the situation for everyone, or inflame the situation.'
'Everyone's uncomfortable with the way things are. I want to resolve it so that we can work together, but I don't know how. What would you do, Mr B?'
'Sometimes when I know I'm going to have to deal with a conflict with another person, I work it through in my head first, and practise what I'm going to say and do. Would you find it useful if we had a go at doing that?'

Kelly agreed, and Glenn spent a little bit of time helping her to imagine what she would feel, see, hear and do at her next small group meeting. Using role play, they then went on to work through what might happen, with Glenn saying things like, 'If you said that to me this is how I might respond.' Through rehearsal, Kelly was able to work out a constructive strategy for resolving her conflict.

Classroom leaders:
▼ Invite responsible choice-making
▼ Model using self-talk
▼ Include the use of multi-modal strategies
▼ Capitalize on opportunities presented by conflict

▼ *PUTTING GLENN IN HIS PLACE* ▼

It was a hot Friday afternoon, and Kelly, who was chairperson that day, had just asked, 'Has anyone else got anything to say?' in preparation for closing the meeting, when the bell went.

Glenn stood up and said, 'Can everybody make sure that all the chairs are put back, and the whiteboard — then off you go.'

Everyone started to move, except Kelly, who remained seated and said, 'Excuse me, could everybody please come back and sit down for a minute — I've got something else to say.'

Everyone came back and sat down, including Glenn. Kelly looked around the circle and said, 'I'd like to formally close the meeting if nobody has any points to bring up, and if we could all help to put the gear away, then we may be able to go.'

This was the moment when Glenn well and truly knew that his role had changed! His main thought was, 'We've succeeded!'

Classroom leaders:
▼ Develop mutually high expectations
▼ Work to develop learner responsibility
▼ Share leadeship and responsiblity

▼ *MAKING CONNECTIONS* ▼

The meeting had reached the agenda item marked 'Adviser's comments'. That meant it was Glenn's turn. He began: 'I'd like to use my time today for us to do some further thinking and talking about what we are learning or feel we are gaining from our project.'

Kelly spoke first. 'I just feel that what we are learning is really real, and I'm enjoying it a lot.'
Julie joined in. 'I'm really enjoying maths a lot more because working in the budget group has helped me realize that a lot of the maths we do actually *is* going to be useful when I leave school.'
'It's really helped my English,' added Enzo. 'I'm getting much better at writing letters to different sorts of people.'
'I reckon it's great,' Rachael said 'I've been teaching my mum a lot of the skills I'm learning in the promotions group and it's really helping to get her windcheater business going.'

There was a pause. Paul spoke quietly and thoughtfully. 'I reckon I've learned some things about myself — like, I like working in a group but I can talk more and give more ideas if I've had some time to think things through on my own first.'

'I'm really pleased to hear your comments,' said Glenn, 'and I'm certainly impressed by your journal reflections as well. You're learning more about yourselves, and you're making lots of connections between different subjects and the outside world. These are very powerful and important things to learn.'

'What about you, Mr B? What are you learning?' smiled Tim.
'Heaps,' answered Glenn. 'In fact I'd like to make my journal writings available for you to read. I guess one specific thing I've been doing a lot of thinking about is assessment, and how it *has* to describe the competencies you're gaining as part of what you're learning. One thing you've helped me realize is how capable kids are of dealing with their own assessment. In fact, staff have been talking about this a lot and we're working on developing more appropriate forms of assessment across the board.'

Glenn looked around and said, 'Well, my time-slot is certainly up! One thing I'd like you to think about some more, though, is the specific competencies and skills you're learning and how they relate to different subject areas. We'll discuss these during reflection time, period 4 next Thursday.'

Classroom leaders:
▼ Engage learners in ongoing reflection
▼ Encourage personal connection-making
▼ Give meaningful praise
▼ Involve learners in their own assessment
▼ Foster learning transfer to other situations
▼ Model their own reflection and learning

Reflecting on learning

This experience will always be with us
for future reference in tomorrow's
society. It is a great feeling to achieve
something without the direct help
of the teachers - I have gained much
more confidence in myself, and I
understand a lot more now about
learning. I love it.

Kelly Brown
Student

What I see happening is that students are now
taking far more responsibility for their own
learning. They are developing a great deal
of respect for the ideas and experience
of others and they are being most resourceful
in meeting their needs in new and real situations.
These young people are developing skills and
qualities that are just as important as the old
3 r's and skills that they will need every day
to be successful in the society of the future.

Jill Davis
Parent and Project Adviser

In all the years I've been teaching, I don't think I've ever seen students so motivated and enthusiastic. It wasn't because of the money we made - we operated on a money-go-round basis where the profit went back to the group and the school as a resource to be used for further learning activities

I believe that if you present 'making money' to students as the key motive it will become the key motivation. If you think students can't be motivated by anything else, it doesn't say much for students or teachers.

The real profit was in the learning - what we all learned about was the capacity of students to manage their own learning, to become effective thinkers, negotiators and communicators in enterprising and co-operative ways.

Through participating in this project my students now have the skills to plan for, and face, the future with confidence and with a strong sense of personal direction. I know that I have also changed and grown to be stronger as a member of our profession.

I know that as a teacher I have done my job well.

Glenn Bromfield
Teacher and Project Adviser

Isn't this what we want for ourselves as teachers? To feel as enthusiastic and empowered by learning as our students, and to feel proud to be a member of the teaching profession.

And isn't this what we want for our students? To have them develop positive lifelong attitudes to learning, to take increasing responsibility for their own learning, to be able to share responsibility with others, and to have them begin to see that they can shape their own futures through education.

The kind of learning undertaken in this classroom — its authentic, purposeful nature, its co-operative approach and use of democratic processes in ways that include and challenge all learners, and the partnership approach between home, school and community — is not an isolated example.

We have seen such empowerment in action in a myriad of ways in the classrooms of many great teachers we've been fortunate enough to work with, both across Australia and internationally. Whilst the ages of the learners and the contexts vary a great deal, what these teachers have in common is a principle-centred approach. They work continuously at understanding these principles and at applying them to their own particular situations, and they engage in ongoing reflection about their own learning.

On the following three pages, we have brought together the effective learning and teaching principles embedded in the Campbelltown story, and invite you to engage in some personal reflection as a result of reading it. Because we know that preferences differ, we have provided a structured reflection and a completely open-ended one.

As teacher, as leader and as learner, remember to affirm yourself in terms of what you are already doing, to focus on the principles of what you are learning, and to think about how these principles transfer into your particular situation.

To empower growth in others

▼ Provide real think-time
▼ Promote engagement in authentic, purposeful learning
▼ Offer open-ended learning opportunities
▼ Understand that learning need to be enjoyable
▼ Build from what learners know and can do
▼ Explain the purpose
▼ Make use of visual organizers
▼ Encourage thinking in metaphor
▼ Take time to support individuals
▼ Give feedback on observations
▼ Help realistic goal-setting
▼ Encourage learners to ask their own questions and seek their own answers
▼ Share your power with others
▼ Use a variety of strategies
▼ Foster learning with and from peers
▼ Develop understandings of many ways of learning
▼ Appreciate the importance of imagination in learning
▼ Help learners to use the metacognitive cycle of plan-monitor-evaluate
▼ Help learners to develop context appropriate strategies
▼ Understand the importance of risk-taking in learning
▼ Focus on learner self-evaluation
▼ Develop learner responsibility to self and others
▼ Reframe mistake-making
▼ Invite responsible choice-making

▼ Model using self-talk
▼ Include the use of multi-modal strategies
▼ Captitalize on opportunities presented by conflict
▼ Develop mutually high expectations
▼ Work to develop learner responsibility
▼ Share leadership and responsibility
▼ Engage learners in ongoing reflection
▼ Encourage personal connection-making
▼ Give meaningful praise
▼ Involve learners in their own assessment
▼ Foster learning transfer to other situations
▼ Model your own reflection and learning

Reflecting on empowerment in action

▼ Reading this section reinforced for me:

▼ One thing I learned from the Campbelltown story is:

▼ The most significant principle in this section for me is:

▼ One challenge I will set myself now is:

Notes and thoughts ▼ ▼ ▼

Walk the leader's walk

Every exceptional leader is a learner

In working towards principle-centred teaching, we need to acknowledge the powerful connections between teaching and leadership, the significance of our role, and understand the principles which are integral to effective leadership.

Many fine teachers we know actually put these principles into practice intuitively, that is, without consciously thinking about the principles themselves. However, when we take more conscious control over what we do and how we do it, we become meta-teachers — more self-aware and more effective because of it.

Teachers who are truly leaders are able to integrate both. They develop an awareness of key leadership principles, and 'walk the leader's walk' by modelling it in practice.

▼ *DEALING WITH COMPLEX ROLES* ▼

As part of their professional development program in 1990, members of the Tasmanian Association of Senior Staff developed a list of the roles they played during any ordinary school day. They did this as a way of acknowledging the increasing complexity of a teacher's role, and were surprised by the size of the list, which included . . .

---

counsellor, mediator, learner, communicator, mentor, psychologist, administrator, social worker, confidante, negotiator, innovator, organizer, judge, jury, go-between, interior decorator, coach, resource manager, diplomat, supervisor, bus driver, reporter, PR person, philosopher, researcher, parent liaison, chauffeur, buyer, carer, friend, co-ordinator, keyboard operator, motivator, inspector, finance manager, inspirer, participant, telephonist, secretary, leader, planner, cleaner, scribe, host, storyteller, team member, actor, office assistant, encourager, aide, teacher. . .

The development of this list prompted further discussion about the specific and changing role of both teachers and students in classrooms. One teacher, Anne, described to the group how this issue had been explored with some Year 9 students:

'Students worked in small groups, discussing statements from the board, and the teacher wrote from her perspective, too. It looked something like this', and Anne wrote the following:

The students discussed . . .	*The teacher wrote about . . .*
Things that will help me to learn better in class are . . .	Things that will help me enjoy teaching in this class are . . .
The role of the teacher is . . .	The role of the students is . . .
The role of the students is . . .	The role of the teacher is . . .

Anne concluded, 'They gathered all the ideas and then worked together to establish a set of clear guidelines and expectations for the future operation of the class.'

Classroom leaders:
 ▼ Acknowledge the complexity of their role
 ▼ Clarify roles and expectations

▼ ENVISIONING THE FUTURE ▼

Mrs Blackhurst asked us to think about the future and what might be important to learn. We interviewed partners and we all shared our ideas. These are the ideas we came up with:

> • Solve problems
> • think for ourselves
> • use our imaginations
> • listen to others
> • communicate with people
> • co-operate with others
> • make responsible choices
> • accept other ideas as worthwhile
> • care about the feelings of others
> • learn to use our spare time
> • believe in ourselves
> • discipline ourselves to do our work
> • remember that education is for life

Year 5/6 Upper Burnie P.S.

Classroom leaders:
▼ Are clear about what they value
▼ Develop a shared vision for what learning and education can be

▼ *AIMING HIGH* ▼

It was Monday morning, and Janet had just finished telling her class the story of Walt Disney, his life and his dream.

'Walt Disney achieved a lot in his life, and he also made a contribution to our world,' said Janet. 'What sorts of beliefs, or qualities or skills do you think he had that enabled him to do that?'

'Well, he didn't let things stop him,' responded Harry. 'Even when he got fired from that newspaper and was told his ideas were no good, he kept going.'

'He must have had a fantastic imagination,' said Kylie.

'Yeah, he had the ideas,' agreed Shane, 'but, like, he didn't build Disneyland himself — he must have been able to work with a lot of other people.'

More ideas were shared, and Janet wrote them all on the board. Then she wrote in large writing:

> # If you can dream it, you can do it.

'If we look at your ideas,' she said, indicating the list on the board, 'we can see that they reflect one of Walt Disney's key beliefs. This belief,' and she pointed to the quote, 'certainly helped him to achieve success. What I'd like you to do now is to have a think about what this belief means to *you*. You might like to talk about it with another person first — but then I'd like you to write it in your journal as our quote for the week. Use it as the basis to set one or two goals for yourself.'

Classroom leaders:
▼ Introduce learners to role models
▼ Believe in learners and help learners to believe in themselves
▼ Make explicit the skills needed for success

▼ *BEING ORGANIZED* ▼

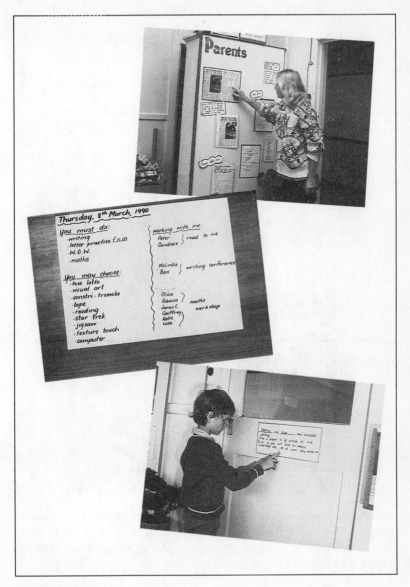

Classroom leaders:
▼ Are organised

▼ *LAYING FOUNDATIONS* ▼

'My priority for this year is to create a truly learning-effective, co-operative classroom. I'm fairly clear about how that classroom will look and function. What I need to do is think through a plan for the first day, and the first week, so that I can begin building first steps for a very solid foundation.'

Classroom leaders:
▼ Think big, start small

▼ *INFLUENCING OTHERS* ▼

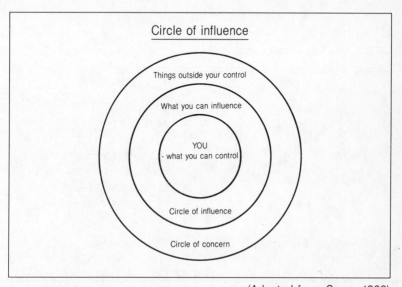

(Adapted from Covey 1989)

Everyone has a range of concerns. Some of those we can control or influence, others rest outside our sphere of influence. The important thing is how we deal with those concerns.

Pro-active people focus their energies on the things they can do something about. As they do this, the nature of their positive energy spreads, causing their circle of influence to actually enlarge.

Reactive people, on the other hand, spend their time and energy focusing on circumstances over which they have no control. Their focus results in blaming and feeling victimized and powerless because the nature of their energy causes their circle of influence to shrink.

Classroom leaders:
▼ Work on what they can influence

▼ *THINKING WIN–WIN* ▼

Consider the different responses in the way the issue of Monday yard duty is handled here:

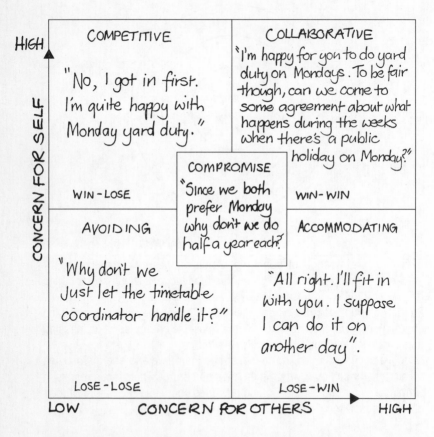

When the issue is important to both parties, everyone's needs are more likely to be satisfied through a collaborative approach.

Classroom leaders:
▼ Think win-win

▼ *APPROACHING THINGS POSITIVELY* ▼

Consider the difference between these two examples:

Reactive teacher	Pro-active teacher
focuses on the past, attaches blame	looks to the future
'Gosh Johnny's lazy.'	'Johnny's a real challenge to teach.'
'Stop talking and get on with your work.'	'You have 10 minutes left. What do you need to do to get finished?'
'On Wednesday she spat at Mrs Jones and on Thursday she kicked . . .	'Let's list the positive behaviours, no matter how small, that we've observed in Jenny this week.'
'Damn! We can't have the room we wanted in order to watch the video.'	'We need to change our plans for this session. Although we can't watch the video, we're lucky it's such a sunny day we can work on our outside investigation.'
'Why did you . . .? You shouldn't have done that.'	'That was awful! I know you can do better. Next time I'd like you to ...'

Pro-active teachers set out what is wanted in advance and lead the way to it.

Classroom leaders:
▼ Choose to think, act and speak positively

▼ *DEALING WITH CHANGE* ▼

The biggest challenge for me in working with the Campbelltown students was keeping up with the pace at which students accepted the responsibility of their new roles as the major decision-makers and managers of their own learning. In fact, the pace of this learning was unlike any other that I had encountered. I found the resultant pressure and challenge for rapid adaptation of my role scary at first. My initial role of 'teacher up front' and 'director of intellectual traffic' changed variously to, and between, that of adviser, observer, facilitator, confidante and counsellor.

Although initially somewhat apprehensive about not having the usual amount of control over the path student learning was to take, I suppose, like the students in the group, I could feel the excitement and the positive feeling for learning that was being generated.

I could sense that for me something quite different and exciting was already happening. I just knew that something really powerful was emerging and that I should encourage it and learn from its development.

Glenn Bromfield
Teacher.

Classroom leaders:
▼ Have a positive orientation toward change
▼ Trust their intuition
▼ Co-create knowledge with other learners

▼ *KEEPING A SENSE OF HUMOUR* ▼

Peter, the district superintendent, while making his first visit to a school which had felt the brunt of the previous year's government budget cuts, met up with Grant in the staffroom. 'Hi Grant, how are things?'
Grant replied, 'I'm all fired up, full of inspiration and enthusiasm and looking forward to a great year.'
Peter, looking pleased, commented, 'It sounds as if you're off to a great start, then', to which Grant retorted, 'Nah — I'm just joking — but in this climate if I can't keep a sense of humour I'll go under.'
'Well,' said Peter, 'I'm glad you're still smiling. You know, I was reading something just last week which suggested that one predictor of success for students was found to be the amount of shared laughter in the staffroom on the first day of school[*]. So if you're maintaining your sense of humour, it sounds as if your kids might be off to a good start anyway!'

Laughter, maintaining a sense of humour, and using humour appropriately, are essential for promoting a sense of community, and for the expression of creativity as well as helping learning to be more enjoyable.
As teachers we need to work to:
- *laugh with learners rather than at them*
- *use humour to build rapport rather than destroy it*
- *defuse situations with humour rather than exacerbate them*
- *use humour to enhance creativity rather than inhibit it*

---

[*] From a study conducted by the National Association of Secondary School Principals in America

Classroom leaders:
▼ Understand the importance of humour
▼ Use humour appropriately with others

▼ *INTEGRATING LEARNING* ▼

Roxanne, Eric, Tony and Dot were discussing the thinking skills program that their school had bought 'on approval'.

'It looks great,' said Roxanne. 'And teaching kids how to become effective thinkers and problem solvers is going to be absolutely critical to the way they live in the future.'

'I agree.' Eric skimmed the page with his finger. 'And there seems to be a wide range of thinking skills covered in here. What do you think, Dot?'

'I don't dispute what you've both said ... I'm just a bit concerned about time — or lack of it — to teach all the things we need to teach.'

Tony spoke up. 'Maybe we can look at this in a slightly different way. Instead of *adding* a thinking skills program — and I have a concern about 'separate programs' that have no meaningful connection with what we do already — I think we could find a way to integrate the skills.' Everyone was listening, and Tony continued. 'For example, we could cross-check the skills and processes in this program with the thinking skills and processes which are inherent across our existing curriculum.'

'That would overcome my concern about time,' said Dot, 'and it might also help me to become clearer about the sorts of thinking skills and processes I need to make explicit to kids.'

The group agreed to do some individual thinking and tackle this at their next meeting. 'You're right about time, Dot,' Tony remarked. 'There's never enough of it! The bell's just about to go.'

The bell rang and students began to arrive in the classroom where they'd been meeting. 'It's good modelling for the kids to see us working this way,' concluded Roxanne. 'After all, we can't expect them to work together unless we do it as well.'

Classroom leaders:
  ▼ Integrate, rather than add, concepts and ideas
  ▼ Walk the walk rather than talk the talk

▼ *KEEPING COMMITMENTS* ▼

'Miss Armstrong, Miss Armstrong, look what Henry's brought,' clamoured the little entourage accompanying Henry. Denise Armstrong peeped into the box that Henry was carrying, looked at Henry's shining eyes, and felt the children's excitement.

She smiled at the children. 'Well, I did promise that when Henry's mouse had its babies we would focus our learning around mice. Instead of going on with our contract work this morning, let's spend some time looking at and talking about them.

'We can get lots of books from the library about mice,' said Henry, 'because I've been reading them.'

'Great.' said Denise. 'And maybe we could make a wall story, and you might also like to do some writing of your own.'

Which they did ... and, in fact, when the senior teacher arrived to work with her reading group she found children not only talking, reading and writing about mice, but exploring possible maths and science investigations which could be related to mice.

'This looks exciting, Denise!' smiled Peta. 'My reading group hasn't even noticed I've arrived. They usually meet me at the door!'

'We put our contract work aside today,' Denise responded. 'When kids are this excited about learning, I find I have to be flexible with our regular program.'

'And the kids certainly appreciate that,' said Peta. 'What I notice, though, is that whilst you're flexible, you maintain consistency with important learning principles — just look at the real and purposeful learning going on! 'Well' she added, as she moved off to find the children in her reading group, 'I guess I'll be learning a lot more about mice this morning!'

Classroom leaders:
▼ Follow through and keep commitments
▼ Use the teachable moments
▼ Are flexible and consistent

▼ *THINKING GLOBALLY* ▼

Classroom leaders:
▼ Have a global view

▼ *MAINTAINING PROFESSIONALISM* ▼

In the staffroom at lunchtime Monique was steaming over Terry's inability to get to class on time and his patronizing attitude towards the students. She was fed up with having to deflect comments from students and parents. As she sat at her desk musing over what to do, she picked up her journal and looked at what she had written as her personal code of ethics. She read:

All people with whom I come in contact deserve respect as unique individuals, with and from whom I can learn. I will demonstrate this respect in my actions, my thoughts and my words.

As she reread this, Monique concluded that in order to maintain integrity for both herself and Terry she needed to confront him in a positive and constructive way, and so she decided to wait until she had calmed down.

The following day she sought support from the deputy principal in dealing with what she saw as an issue of professional ethics. Vic indicated his position. 'I value loyalty, honesty and professional behaviour Monique, and I'm prepared to discuss your concerns as long as we do take them to Terry in a positive way. I know I would appreciate that from others.'

Together they discussed ways to achieve this and planned a course of action. Vic then expanded the discussion by suggesting that, since there appeared to be no generally agreed code of ethics across the teaching profession, it might be useful to pursue the notion of developing a creed for their school, through discussion at a future staff forum.

Classroom leaders:
▼ Commit to a professional code of ethics
▼ Display integrity and personal dignity

▼ *LEADING BEYOND THE CLASSROOM* ▼

Our school community believes that when student problems arise, they need to be sorted out. It's not about punishment — it's about time and support.

To this end, we have set up a sorting-out room where we all take turns at lunchtime, on a roster basis, to support children in sorting out behaviour management issues that occur during playground breaks.

Our focus is to help children to resolve their conflicts by supporting them to assert themselves, and through negotiating conciliation. It's given us the opportunity to practise, and model, processes that are consistent with our behaviour management policy. This has led to training for peer support and mediation — it has given students a model to work with themselves.

A direction for the future is for the school to train and use parents to help mediate in 'sorting-out' situations, and the beginnings of this are our plans to video the sorting-out process for parents to take home, and view. What better way to help them learn skills to deal with behaviour management issues differently?

Collaborative reflection by Mansfield Park Primary School Staff

CHILD/CHILDREN INVOLVED .... CLASS/ES ....**12**..........

.........**Belinda Room 12**...

.........**Christina Room 12**...

Time of incident: **Over past few days**   Date:**26/3/92**

Sent by: ......**J. Coats**..

Please circle the appropriate code below and give brief details if necessary:

HARASSMENT	
Teasing	T
Sexual	SH
Racial	RH
Following	F
Friendship issues	FR
(e.g. I won't be your friend)	

NON-COMPLIANCE	
Rules: Out of bounds	O/B
Toilets	T
Sprinklers/water	W
Bells	B
Damage to property	D
Stealing (incl. food)	N/C
With teacher instructions	N/C

AGGRESSION	
Play fighting	P
Threatening behaviour	TH
Deliberate hurting	DH
Abusive language	L

UNSAFE PLAY	
Climbing	U
Dangerous objects	UO
(e.g. sand)	

Brief details of incident:

Will need to S.O.P - The boys are concerned about the girls telling other students that they are going out with them, following them around and asking for their address. They have asked them to stop but the girls have continued to harass.

'Sorting-out' slip, Mansfield Park PS

Classroom leaders:
▼ Make a leadership contribution beyond the classroom

▼ *FEELING GOOD ABOUT TEACHING* ▼

Belinda's diary   6th April

I went to a seminar with Ralph the other night which was aimed at business and industry leaders. What struck me was that the sorts of things the presenter was talking about as essential leadership skills - things like establishing shared goals, involving others in decision-making, giving feedback, helping people learn teamwork and interpersonal skills and so on - are the same things that I do regularly in the classroom. It certainly made me aware that as teachers we need to recognise and value the skills that we do have. It helped me feel really good about being a teacher.

Classroom leaders:
  ▼ Are aware of their leadership skills and are proud to be teachers

True classroom leaders work from a highly professional frame of reference — they try to build congruence between their ideal pictures, their thoughts and their behaviours. They understand the positive and powerful impact this has on their students, their colleagues, their school community, and, ultimately, their own lives as teachers.

And they continually monitor what they think and do in terms of the principles they adhere to by engaging in ongoing reflection. You might like to use the following three pages to engage in your own reflection. Look at the listing of leadership principles, think through their application for you, and make a commitment to further your own leadership development.

To walk the leader's walk

- ▼ Acknowledge the complexity of your role
- ▼ Clarify roles and expectations
- ▼ Be clear about what you value
- ▼ Develop a shared vision for what learning and education can be
- ▼ Introduce learners to role models
- ▼ Believe in learners and help learners to believe in themselves
- ▼ Make explicit the skills needed for success
- ▼ Be organized
- ▼ Think big, start small
- ▼ Work on what you can influence
- ▼ Think win-win
- ▼ Choose to think, act and speak positively
- ▼ Have a positive orientation toward change
- ▼ Trust your intuition
- ▼ Co-create knowledge with other learners
- ▼ Understand the importance of humour
- ▼ Ue humour appropriately
- ▼ Integrate, rather than add, concepts and ideas
- ▼ Walk the walk rather than talk the talk
- ▼ Follow through and keep commitments
- ▼ Use the teachable moments
- ▼ Be both flexible and consistent
- ▼ Have a global view
- ▼ Commit to a professional code of ethics
- ▼ Display integrity and personal dignity
- ▼ Make a leadership contribution beyond the classroom
- ▼ Be aware of your leadership skills and be proud to be a teacher

Reflecting on walking the leader's walk

▼ I believe that I implement the following principles very well in my role as a teacher:

▼ One goal I will set for my personal development is:

▼ To help me achieve this I need to:

▼ I plan to begin working on this:

I will review my progress toward achieving this goal on _____ and have noted this in my diary.

Notes and thoughts

Build relationships with others

Schools are not buildings
curriculum timetables and meetings.
Schools are relationships and
interactions among people.

— *Johnson and Johnson, 1989*

Principle-centred teaching acknowledges the critical importance of realtionship in learning. The environment we create, the curriculum experiences we provide, and the organizational strategies we use, only support what we are, what we model, and the relationships we build. Learning and education is about people, and taking the time to build positive and strong interpersonal relationships is the key that unlocks the door to lifelong learning.

▼ *LEARNING BY LISTENING* ▼

Glenn Bromfield worked on the premise of seeking first to understand and then to be understood. In his interaction with students at Campbelltown District High School he chose to practise active and empathic listening skills before offering his opinions, ideas and thoughts, and to encourage the students by asking a few carefully-worded questions.

Classroom leaders:
▼ Listen more and talk less
▼ Talk with people rather than at them

▼ *BEING PERCEPTIVE* ▼

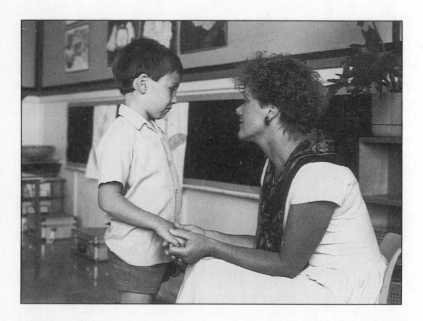

'You seem to be looking a bit 'down' today Ben. Would you like to talk about it?' Mary-Ann Griggs asked quietly.

'My dog got run over last night,' sniffed Ben, tears threatening to overwhelm.

'That must have been awful for you,' acknowledged Mary-Ann. 'Are you okay to join the listening post group — or would you like some time to yourself for a little while?'

Ben nodded at the latter suggestion and Mary-Ann settled him into a bean-bag with a promise to return in a few minutes.

Classroom leaders:
▼ Notice and acknowledge others' feelings
▼ Acknowledge many aspects of people's lives
▼ Attend to the little things as well as the big things

▼ *SEEKING CONGRUENCE* ▼

When we work to empower learners and foster a team approach, we need to understand that up to 80**%** of the messages we give are non-verbal.

Consider the different 'power' messages that these two classroom arrangements provide:

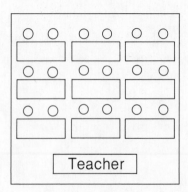 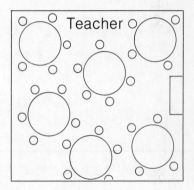

The physical set up of the room, the language we use and the non-verbal messages we convey, all need to be congruent to achieve consistency in our classrooms.

Classroom leaders:
▼ Give congruent messages
▼ Understanding the power of non-verbal messages

▼ *SHARING ONESELF* ▼

A page from Denise Armstrong's interaction classroom journal:

Tonight I've promised to look after a little baby who lives round the corner from me. His name is Samuel and I'm pretty sure he is about 15 months old.

He's quite a cute little fellow, but he always wants me to read him stories and 'play blocks with him. ⚡ I hope he doesn't cry too much and I hope his mum CHANGES HIS NAPPY before she goes out. I've only ever changed about 5 nappies in my entire life. I'm not, what you'd call, a super dooper baby sitter.

What will I do to entertain the monster if he wakes up during the night? What if his nappy needs to be changed? Don't worry. Miss Armstrong

Change his nappy with a peg on your nose! (kerry)

change them I can do it Adam

EEK! put sticky tape over His mouth if He cries.

because I've never changed a nappy in my like before either! Marion

Tell him to cross his legs B.Burley

I don't know how Dianne

give him a bottle! Kt'lr y Melissa Slater Mark

Ht I wold put er rubber gloves on Almira.

change it and read him a story so he will go back to sleep Nicole

Classroom leaders:
▼ Share something of themselves with others

▼ *BUILDING COMMITMENT* ▼

Neil Bolton's Year 4 class had spent considerable time during a morning, developing rules and responsibilities for their eagerly awaited camp which was due to take place the following week.

They had individually written down their ideas, discussed them in small groups, presented a summary of their ideas, and negotiated class agreement on the rules and responsibilities they thought were the most important. Neil had written the final lists on the board as a visual reflection of students' ideas.

'Now that we have agreed on clear responsibilities,' said Neil, pointing to the appropriate list, 'it is your responsibility to carry them out. Remember,' he emphasised, 'it is *your* camp. The decisions you make will determine its success. So, what I'd like you to do now is move back into your camp teams and negotiate with your team members how these responsibilities will be fairly shared.'
'Since it's such a lovely day,' he continued, 'some teams might like to work in our outside area. I know that if you run into any difficulties, you'll ask for help . . .' As Neil quietly moved between groups, observing and listening to comments such as 'I'll do any job but the dishes,' and 'What about Aldo — he hasn't got a job yet,' he smiled, and knew that the camp would be a success. After all, the commitment to make it such was there.

Classroom leaders:
▼ Invite others' ideas and act on them
▼ Demonstrate trust

▼ *UNDERSTANDING HUMAN NEEDS* ▼

As human beings we are all driven by an overwhelming need to make sense of the world in the best possible way that we can. We carry pictures in our heads and our hearts of what and who our ideal world will contain, and it is the difference between this and our reality that leads us to think, feel, respond and behave in different ways. In living and working with others we need to understand that all behaviour is purposeful and can be changed if we so choose. This is the essence of helping students learn self-responsibility. If we accept this and acknowledge that all behaviour is that person's best attempt, in the only way they know how, based on their knowledge, their experience, their influences, their morality and their values to meet their basic physical and psychological needs (of belonging, empowerment, freedom of choice and fun), we are then well placed to support the process of developing postitive, self-responsible learning and behaviour through the setting of achievable goals.

Many effective teachers either consciously or intuitively find the following needs-based framework useful in the development of a collaborative classroom and responsible learning.

Creating a sense of BELONGING • to each other • to the class • to the school • to the community • to the global community	Developing a feeling of EMPOWERMENT • through developing self-control and a sense of self-worth

Understanding physical
SURVIVAL NEEDS

Making provision for EXPANDING CHOICES and MAKING RESPONSIBLE CHOICES • in learning and behaviour	Instilling a LOVE OF LEARNING • through inquiry and self- discovery through ENJOYMENT • of school • of life and learning

Based on the work of Dr William Glasser.

Classroom leaders:
▼ Understand people's basic needs

▼ *DEALING WITH DIFFERENT VIEWPOINTS* ▼

Sue Ryan was preparing her 11- and 12-year-old learners to engage in a controversial discussion around a high-interest issue. She referred to a quote on the board:
'To truly understand another's perspective, take time to walk in their shoes, to see through their eyes.'

Using a think-pair-share co-operative structure, learners considered what they thought it meant, and Sue drew out from their comments the importance of listening to other people's viewpoints and what might be learned from doing this.

'The issue we'll be discussing today', said Sue, 'Is one where people may have different points of view. In order to do what you've just said is important — things like learn from others, gain a more complete picture, and show that you're open-minded — let's consider what taking different viewpoints into account sounds like, looks like, and feels like.'

Drawing a Y-chart on the board, Sue listed students' suggestions, adding in a couple of her own.

'While you're discussing the issue in your teams,' Sue concluded, 'my role will be to act as observer, noting down specific ways you demonstrate this important skill. You might like to use some of the 'hooks' on the Y-chart to help you. I'll give you some feedback when we reflect on how we've done just before recess.'

Feels like:
- listening
- your opinion counts
- it's okay to say your opinion

Looks like:
- looking at the speaker
- leaning forward
- sitting still while listening
- nodding

Sounds like:
- I hadn't thought of it that way before
- I wonder if you have considered...
- You've given me another angle to it.

Classroom leaders:
▼ Promote empathy for others' viewpoints
▼ Explicity develop social skills

▼ *WORKING THINGS THROUGH* ▼

Joel was flicking paper at Joseph across the room. 'Joel, that behaviour is not acceptable in this classroom. Please stop now . . . Thankyou . . . What is it that you're supposed to be doing?' Joel shamefacedly replied, 'These problems, Miss.' 'Well, you haven't signalled for help. Is there something more you need to get started?' Melinda spoke quietly to Joel some five minutes after the rest of the class had started work. Joel looked up with an anxious face. 'I don't understand how to do this algebra and everyone else does. I'm just dumb!' 'Well,' said Melinda, 'Joan found this difficult and I've just been helping her. Would you like me to show you, too?' Joel nodded.

Melinda sat down and went through a problem, modelling self-talk as she did so. 'How about you have a go at it yourself now while I'm here with you.' Joel's next attempt to solve a problem was successful and Melinda observed, 'You've got the right answer. Can you explain back to me what you've done so I can hear that you understand it?' Joel explained, and Melinda prepared to move off saying, 'I'm just going to check that everyone else is okay. You have a go at the next couple, and I'll be back to see how you're doing in 10 minutes. If you need me before that just use our 'I need help' signal and I'll come back as soon as I can.' (Melinda had recognized that many of her secondary students preferred not to seek help overtly, so she had established an unobtrusive non-verbal signal to indicate that they needed her assistance.)

Classroom leaders:
▼ Demonstrate patience
▼ Care enough to confront constructively
▼ Are consistent in the way they treat people

When we are clear about the principles underpinning the building of personal relationships we can work more effectively at our own interpersonal skills and on creating the conditions in which these skills can develop further.

You might like to reflect on these principles, listed on the page following, and reflect on the positive relationships you currently have with learners. At the same time you might like to envision how to achieve more enhanced relationships through a principle-centred approach.

To build relationships with others

- ▼ Listen more and talk less
- ▼ Talk with people rather than at them
- ▼ Notice and acknowledge others' feelings
- ▼ Acknowledge many aspects of people's lives
- ▼ Attend to the little things as well as the big ones
- ▼ Give congruent messages
- ▼ Understand the power of non-verbal messages
- ▼ Share something of yourself with others
- ▼ Invite others' ideas and act on them
- ▼ Demonstrate trust
- ▼ Understand people's basic needs
- ▼ Promote empathy for others' viewpoints
- ▼ Explicity develop social skills
- ▼ Demonstrate patience
- ▼ Care enough to confront constructively
- ▼ Be consistent in the way you treat people

Reflecting on building relationships with others

I feel really happy with the relationships I have with a few/most/all of the students in my classroom this year.

I find it easier to develop positive relationships when:

Some ways in which I can create these conditions include:

The principle I need to work on most in improving my classroom relationships is:

When I achieve this my classroom will:

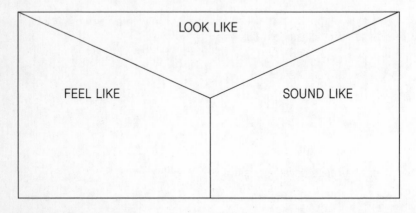

Notes and thoughts

▼
▼
Create

▼
▼
a

▼
▼
community

▼
▼
of

▼
▼
learners

Dependent people need others to get what they want.
Independent people can get what they want
through their own effort.
Interdependent people combine their
own efforts with the efforts of
others to achieve their greatest successes.

Covey, 1989

Our classrooms need to reflect a major challenge that our planet is facing — the challenge of building wholeness and unity in a way that also preserves uniqueness and human differences.

Classroom leaders build a community where self-responsibility and independence go hand-in-hand with shared responsibility, co-operation and interdependence. Moreover, this community includes parents and the broader community as valued partners and rich resources in the learning processes of their children.

▼ BUILDING TEAMWORK ▼

Our classroom responsibilities for JUNE

Display board designers
Kylie
Hing

Attendance checkers
Candace
Kristy-Lee

Librarians
Liam H.
Kim

Florists
Liam L.
Stacey

Domestic engineers
Sally
Tony

Book club co-ordinators
Marie
Rebecca

Meteorologists
Jessie
Richard

Post-people
Darren
Mia

Catering organizers
Karl
Nathan

Blackboard shiners
Olivia
Mr. Kyriacou

Notice distributors
Belinda
Adam

Marine biologists
Nick
Georgia

Class goal writers
Kate
Simon

Graphic artists
Katrina
Ben

Message couriers
Theo
Sam

Zookeepers
Kristy S.
Jim

Classroom leaders
▼ Build a class team
▼ Ensure that each person has a part to play

▼ *DESIGNING THE ENVIRONMENT* ▼

Classroom leaders:
▼ Create a stimulating classroom environment

▼ *GOING ROUND CORNERS* ▼

Teacher Narelle Kidson asked learners to reflect at the conclusion of a class meeting on why sitting in a circle might be important. Lots of reasons were suggested, but the following reflection from a nine-year-old girl really made her stop and think:

> "Sitting in a circle is important because we all go round corners in life and this way we can face them together."

It made us stop and think, too!

Classroom leaders:
▼ Have a 'circle' philosophy

▼ *VALUING EXPLICITNESS* ▼

Julie was pleased that she'd arrived early to talk with Di Tait. She was looking forward to being part of Di's Year 5/6 class again. 'One of the things I love about this class is the way in which its culture is made so explicit,' Julie thought, as her glance fell on a large wall chart with the heading 'What we value as learners.' At the bottom of all the writings were thirty signatures, of which Di's was one.

Learners had obviously been engaging in discussion about the advantages and disadvantages of individual, competitive and co-operative learning, and Di was recording their conclusions on the blackboard. She had just recorded Andrew's report when he raised his hand a second time.
'Yes, Andrew,' acknowledged Di. 'Is there something you'd like to add?'
'Yes, Mrs Tait. You're, ah, modelling mistake-making again _____ isn't spelt that way,'
'Oh,' said Di, as her eyes met Julie's, 'maybe we can double-check with a dictionary.' Lots of willing helpers confirmed with their dictionaries that Andrew was right, and the word was corrected . . .

'I haven't heard kids talking about "modelling mistake-making" before,' chuckled Julie, as she and Di walked towards the staffroom at recess.
'It's a term we've talked about as a part of our learning,' responded Di. 'I try to talk with kids and build a language that everybody understands. I feel really comfortable that the kids understand and can use that language. They're certainly good at it — as you saw today!'

Classroom leaders:
▼ Make explicit what is valued
▼ Build a common language

▼ *FINDING SOLUTIONS TOGETHER* ▼

Fiona Jarvis was concerned about the lack of space in her small classroom and the impact it was having on the development of a collaborative class. Having spent considerable time developing consistent classroom procedures and twice rearranging the furniture in ways she believed would promote a more collaborative atmosphere, she chose a Monday morning to share the problem with her Year 6 students.

'What I'd like us to do is push all the desks and tables right out of the way and just sit in the space we've created and talk about this,' was one of two suggestions she made. The second was, 'In your language teams, I'd like you to list the things you see as important in creating a co-operative working space in this room.'

The students generated their lists and then, as a whole class, followed through on a student's suggestion and engaged in a CAF (Consider All Factors - from de Bono CORT Thinking) to determine what was feasible.

As a class they then negotiated where they would like their individual desks to be clustered and how they would like the room organized. John, a student who acknowledged that he worked much better on his individual work when by himself, tucked his desk away in a corner, while agreeing to participate more in class discussions.

For the remainder of the morning, the classroom was a hive of activity, with people moving desks and tables, checking that they had been put in the right place, collecting equipment that hadn't been returned to cupboards, and labelling everything to make it easier to find.

Lunchtime arrived and they proudly invited the principal, Kevin, in to see their revamped classroom, while explaining that this was a six-week trial, to be reviewed at the end of that time. All agreed that the exercise was extremely worthwhile, and that they all felt happy about the result because, as one of the students put it, 'we did it ourselves.'

Classroom leaders:
▼ Spend time developing consistent procedures
▼ Engage learners in evaluating aspects of classroom life
▼ Invite shared decision-making

▼ *APPRECIATING DIFFERENCE* ▼

On entering Christopher Nichols' classroom, Joan felt a stirring of real excitement at the way in which it reflected effective use of space, colour, displays, furniture arrangement and learning centres. Small teams of nine- and ten-year-old learners were engaged purposefully in language experiences, integrated strongly with the arts.

Joan noticed that open-ended challenges had been constructed to encourage learning through as many modes as possible — challenges which invited sensing, feeling, thinking, intuiting, talking, listening, writing, reading, drawing, computing, role playing, making, composing, researching . . . the list grew long as she jotted down observations in her journal.

One team was busily putting the finishing touches to a very large letter-box they'd made in response to a learning centre option:

Plan together and design something that will
help people in our classroom to:

— *appreciate each other more*
— *work on their writing*

Joan observed that each team member was contributing in different ways and asked Chris to tell her a little about the children. He quietly indicated each learner: 'That's Mike — he's using his calligraphy skills to good effect in making the letter-box sign. Ng and Maria are painting the letter-box. That's our integration aide, Mrs Berry, with Maria — you can see that she's using the opportunity to teach Maria particular spatial concepts. Ng only arrived from Cambodia last month — notice how he's listening to Mrs Berry and Maria? He doesn't miss a trick, and he's picking up English fast.' Chris continued, '. . . And the lass sitting next to Mike is Suzy — Suzy's writing the first letter for the letter-box, explaining to the class its intended use. Each of them will sign it, but Suzy's language is advanced and it's a good challenge for her.'

Joan was intrigued. 'Chris, their level of co-operation and task engagement is impressive — what do they actually understand about the way they're working?'

'Why don't you ask them?' smiled Chris, as he was led off by two enthusiastic writers to the conferencing corner. So Joan did. Sitting with the group, she asked, 'I'm wondering what you're learning from working this way.' Suzy answered first. 'We're learning how to work with people.'

'Yes,' agreed Mike. 'You learn about choosing, and sharing ideas. You have to co-operate.'
'Co-operate.' Joan paraphrased. 'What does that mean?'
'I got the boxes and the paints' said Maria proudly.
'I get ruler,' said Ng shyly.
'Yes,' said Suzy. 'Ng's really good at maths, so he did all the calculations and the measuring for our letter-box. We work out our jobs together, 'cos we're all good at different things — we talk about that sometimes with Mr Nichols.' And Mike's final comment was very interesting. 'I love working at centres because you get to use lots of different materials, not just writing in books.'

Classroom leaders:
- ▼ Provide for many modes of learning
- ▼ Encourage the use of learners' strengths
- ▼ Include and challenge all learners
- ▼ Value difference

▼ *BALANCING WAYS OF LEARNING* ▼

'Do we have to do this with other people, or can we do it on our own?' asked 13-year-old Jacqui, of teacher, Tony Ryan.

'Because the task requires a lot of different ideas, I'd like you to work on this in groups of three or four,' explained Tony. 'We're after original ideas here, and what we know about creative thinking is that the more ideas you think of, the more likely it is that really unusual and original ideas will emerge.'

'So today,' Tony continued, 'we need heads together in teams. Over the year you'll have lots of opportunities to work in teams, as well as on your own at times — that's important, too. Sometimes you'll get to choose which way, and sometimes I'll choose, and I'll always try to explain the reasons why.'

'Mr Ryan, I like working with other people, but I enjoy it more if I can choose who I work with.'

This comment came from Abdul.

'I can understand that, Abdul,' smiled Tony. 'There are actually lots of ways we can form groups — I'm wondering, from the way the discussion's going, whether you'd find it useful to spend just a few minutes looking at some of these?'

There were nods, and general agreement was murmured, so Tony explained briefly the three major forms of grouping, and gave a couple of examples of each. 'Okay,' Tony continued. 'Let's do a PMI to brainstorm the pluses and minuses of each.' He drew a quick diagram on the board.

	Group selection		
	Self/friends	Teacher's	Random
P - 'pluses'	_____	_____	_____
M - 'minuses'	_____	_____	_____
I - 'interestings' What to watch for	_____	_____	_____

He went on. 'This will help us to be clear about what we can learn from working in each of these ways, and what we must watch for, or overcome.' Acting as scribe, Tony wrote up all the ideas put forward. The result was enhanced understanding by the class, and Abdul's comment summed up the final discussion nicely: 'I still enjoy working with my friends best but I guess I mightn't learn as much! I suppose I can cope with a dose of all of them, as long as it's fair in the way it's done.'

Classroom leaders:
▼ Keep individual and team learning in balance
▼ Balance the way learning teams are formed

▼ *DEVELOPING PARTNERSHIPS* ▼

Peter, Melanie's new Year 5 teacher, liked to meet with the parents of all his students at the beginning of the year to develop shared goals which they, with the student, might then work on together.

In his meeting with Melanie and her mother, Peter began. 'Mary, what I'd like to do is for each of us to share our hopes for Melanie this year so that we can get the same picture in our heads and all work towards it together.' Mary replied, 'What I want for Melanie this year is for her to really enjoy school and feel happy about coming. I'm a bit worried that she's in a class with a lot of new people and it does take her a long time to make new friends.' 'And what about you, Melanie. What would you like to happen at school this year?' Peter asked.

Melanie looked up. 'I'd really like to make some new friends. All my best friends are back at my other school, and I miss them.'
Peter leaned gently toward her. 'I'd like to help you feel comfortable with the other children too, and help you develop new friendships as much as I can.' He turned back to Mary, and continued. 'Melanie is a very able child, so one of the things I'd like to do is to really extend her thinking and learning. What I would like is for us to find some ways to work together to achieve these things.'

Together they explored a range of possibilities and decided that communication was the most important initial issue for them in monitoring Melanie's progress in class. Peter suggested introducing a special book to provide an on-going dialogue between school and home as a way of sharing her positive experiences, and asked Melanie what she would like to call it. 'Melanie's book!' came the quick response. They decided that Melanie would share the contents of the book with her mother at home twice a week and with Peter during their special 'talk-time' at school.

They ageed that, although initially Peter and Mary would be doing the bulk of the writing, the long-term goal would be to encourage Melanie to use the book herself as a reflection journal to help with their planning.

Classroom leaders:
▼ Develop genuine partnerships with parents
▼ Model inclusive language

▼ *CELEBRATING SUCCESSES* ▼

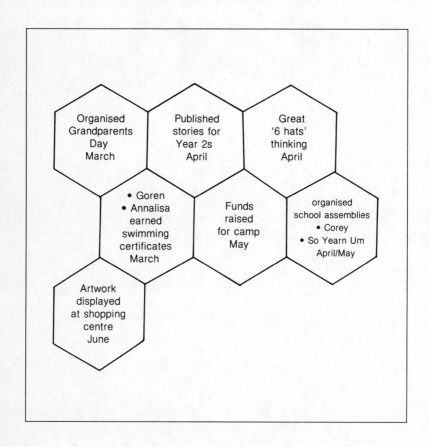

Classroom leaders:
▼ Celebrate indivdual and class successes

▼ *INVOLVING THE WIDER COMMUNITY* ▼

The web shows the community resources and expertise accessed by the students of Campbelltown District High School during their 'Overflow with Info' project.

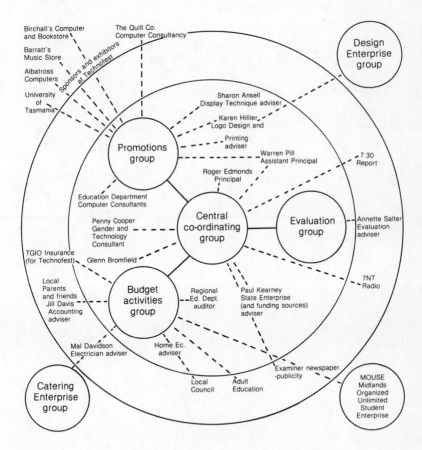

Classroom leaders:
▼ Access the rich learning resources of the community

We as teachers need to have very clear beliefs about what it is that we value so that our actions in our classrooms can model this in practice. It is only when we truly value autonomy that we can build it in our students. It is only when we truly value difference that we can use difference effectively to enrich the learning of all. It is only when we work to include every student that we can build a sense of cohesion in our classroom. And it is only when we value and understand interdependence that we can build a co-operative classroom.

As you peruse the principles on the following page, we invite you to reflect on the congruence between your beliefs and actions, the principles you are currently putting into practice, and aspects you might like to focus on in the future.

To create a community of learners

▼ Build a class team
▼ Ensure that each person has a part to play
▼ Create a stimulating classroom environment
▼ Have a 'circle' philosophy
▼ Make explicit what is valued
▼ Build a common language
▼ Spend time developing consistent procedures
▼ Engage learners in evaluating aspects of classroom life
▼ Invite shared decision-making
▼ Provide for many modes of learning
▼ Encourage the use of learners' strengths
▼ Include and challenge all learners
▼ Value difference
▼ Keep individual and team learning in balance
▼ Balance the way learning teams are formed
▼ Develop genuine partnerships with parents
▼ Model inclusive language
▼ Celebrate individual and class successes
▼ Access the rich learning resources of the community

Reflecting on creating a community of learners

Beliefs I feel most strongly about in creating a community of learners are:

Ways in which I know I am successfully creating a community of learners are:

One principle that I'd like to further develop from this section is:

Some ways I could implement this principle are:

Notes and thoughts

▼ *Work*
▼ *on*
▼ *self-growth*

No one can persuade another to change.
Each of us guards a gate of change that
can only be opened from the inside.

Marilyn Ferguson, 1980

At the heart of the principles surrounding learning and growth is the premise that true power comes from within, rather than from external forces. We must teach from within in order to empower learners. In fact, working from the 'inside-out' is the only way that principle-centred teaching can be successful.

Effective classroom leaders acknowledge the truth of the ancient wisdom: 'To improve others one must first improve oneself.' They work at their leadership skills, at developing a strong sense of self-worth and inner direction, and they commit to working with others in interdependent, collegial ways. For they know that peers are potentially the most powerful source of support and stimulus toward becoming meta-teachers. And they know that they can only assist learners to become what they are capable of if they work on their own self-growth.

▼ *GOING WITHIN: KNOWING ONESELF* ▼

Julie's journal   March 6th.

Today I went down to 15 metres. It was weird sitting on the bottom of the ocean reflecting on the learning processes I had gone through to get to this point. I know that for me the process is the same regardless of whether I'm learning to dive, to program a microwave, or speak in public – I have to actually be given enough information to feel confident to have a go-try a bit, and then think and talk about all the things I did and need to do.

Doing all the diving theory first didn't prepare me for the actual experience of being out of air 10 metres down at all. I think in class sometimes I give the kids too much information and then expect them to be able to just do it. Tomorrow I think I'll try things a little differently.

Maybe one of the things I'll try with the kids is talking with them about what I've learned and then give them more time to think things through first before I expect them to put pen to paper. Figuring out how to do that and keep on task will be interesting.

Classroom leaders:
▼ Work on knowing self
▼ Constantly seek to make links in learning
▼ Affirm themselves
▼ Reflect on their own learning

▼ *GOING WITHIN: INTEGRATING GROWTH* ▼

Julie's journal   March 6th

One thing about being underwater - if you make a mistake you have to rectify it pretty quickly - unless you're like Gill, one of the instructors, of course. Her name is just so appropriate as she's like a fish down there. She really loves diving and it's her enthusiasm that's opened up a whole new world underwater for me.

I'm really looking forward to future adventures. Diving is not only helping me overcome things like fear, panic, claustrophobia and physical limitations. It's also enabling me to use my background in science. And it's providing some real physical balance for all the mental and intellectual work I do. It's just great.

Classroom leaders:
▼ Integrate personal and professional growth
▼ Seek balance in their lives
▼ Show passion for learning and teaching

▼ *MODELLING GROWTH* ▼

As the bell sounded for the end of lunch, Liz and Margaret met at the door of the blackout room and looked at each other with surprised faces.

'What are you doing here, Margaret?' queried Liz. 'I need this room now for the film I'm going to show.'

'Did you check the booking schedule, Liz? I've had the room booked for the past two weeks for this session,' Margaret asserted quietly.

Liz began to look agitated. 'But I need it — I promised the kids — please Margaret — can't you take your kids down to Room 40 — I'll owe you.'

'I understand that you would like the blackout room now,' said Margaret. 'I have, however, planned a practicum session and the students have already set up the equipment. If you give me a bit more notice next time, I'll be happy to negotiate with you.'

Liz turned to her students who were milling around the door with Margaret's students. 'Well kids — I've made a major mistake here. I promised to show you the film this session but I didn't look at the booking schedule and the room was already booked. I'll check and see if it is available tomorrow. In the meantime, let's go to Room 40 as quickly and quietly as we can, and we'll make a start on our written work . . .

Classroom leaders:
▼ Are assertive
▼ Acknowledge their mistakes

▼ *REACHING OUT* ▼

Dale's Journal   May 15th

Well I did it! Tonight after school I achieved something I hadn't thought would be possible for me—I actually prepared and conducted a professional development session for the staff on the maths I've been doing in my classroom. They found it so useful they have asked me to do another one next month. Although I was nervous, I felt really good at being able to share the maths. I've been interested in it for a long time.

Joe and Robyn spoke to me afterwards and suggested that we begin to do some co-planning together, since we all have year 3's and 4's. Now I feel okay about asking Robyn to explain how she uses that social skills chart in her room. I've been wanting to do that with my kids, but I haven't been sure how to go about it.

I think what's really helped me with all this is talking to our deputy principal she's been very supportive and has helped me to realize that it's okay to share ideas and ask for help – that it's part of teaching these days. It was she who suggested that I take a staff meeting on maths.

And I'm feeling great – as if I've had a real shot in the arm about teaching! I'm really looking forward to our first co-planning meeting next Wednesday.

Classroom leaders:
▼ Give and accept peer support
▼ Consciously set out to learn from others
▼ Commit to working with colleagues

▼ *UNDERSTANDING KEY SKILLS* ▼

Some key qualities and skills of people who will lead successfully into the future:

**flexible
adaptable
positive
see change as opportunity
take risks, face the unknown
life-long learners
self-confident
use initiative, innovative
organized active purposeful
negotiate, communicate
plan, problem solve
take responsibility and share responsibility
have a 'we' attitude**

Commission for the Future

Classroom leaders:
▼ Understand key leadership skills

▼ *COACHING EACH OTHER: PLANNING AHEAD* ▼

Judy Stevens and Joan Kreemers were planning a coaching session before school. Together, they taught Year 3 on a time-share basis, but on Wednesdays they co-taught, so this was the day they focused, usually taking turns, on improving their skills through coaching each other. 'This may seem like a small thing, but I really get annoyed with myself for continually responding to the kids with 'good boy' or 'good girl', especially when they're coming up with great ideas,' sighed Joan.

'So what would you like to be able to do?' asked Judy.

'Make my comments more meaningful! As it is now they're meaningless — it's become an automatic response, and the kids know this.' 'What would make it more meaningful for you and for them?' gently probed Judy.

'Well — I guess if my comments were more specific it could give them feedback on the sorts of ideas they come up with, or the kind of thinking they're doing. That might fit with the emphasis we're trying to put on effective thinking with our kids.'

'So, your goal is to respond to kids in more specific ways that give them feedback about the thinking they're actually doing,' checked Judy. Joan nodded, and together they went on to plan a literature session that would provide opportunities for Joan to work on changing her language, and which Judy could observe.

'What kind of responses would you like me to watch for?' Judy asked.

'Maybe comments that say something specific about 'thinking'. Joan paused and thought for a minute. 'Like 'imaginative thinking!' or 'logical reasoning,' or even 'you're using your predicting skills there Barry.' I'll see what pops out but I definitely want to avoid saying 'good', so you might note it down if I do.'

The first bell went, signalling 15 minutes before school began, and Joan and Judy set about preparing for their regular morning session . . .

Classroom leaders:
▼ Constantly seek to improve their learning and teaching
▼ Take risks in their own learning

▼ *COACHING EACH OTHER: BECOMING META-LEARNERS* ▼

'How did you feel the session went?' asked Judy.
'The kids certainly enjoyed *The True Story of the Three Little Pigs,*' commented Joan.

It was 12.15 pm, Joan had taken her literature session late morning, and the children were now busily eating their lunch in class. (Judy and Joan found this a good time-saving 'slot' for debriefing.)
Judy smiled and nodded. Joan continued. 'I was really pleased with the maturity of the discussion that came from the kids, and they seemed intrigued to hear back the sorts of thinking they were doing — I remember three or four specific comments at least that I made. What did you think about it?'
'You asked me to write specific observations today,' Judy responded. 'Would it be useful if we had a look at them now?'

As they went through Judy's jottings, Joan could see that she had, in fact, made a wide range of specific 'thinking' comments to learners. 'Yuk,' Joan grimaced. 'I notice I still used 'good' a couple more times than I thought I had. Having another pair of eyes and ears certainly picks up things that, teaching by myself, I don't notice.'

'I think all this is giving us more conscious control over what we do in the classroom,' Judy volunteered, 'and making us more effective because of it.'
'I think it also parallels what we're trying to do with kids,' added Joan. 'We're trying to help them become more aware of their thinking and take more control over their learning as well. I reckon that's what this 'metacognition' stuff is all about.'

'Your comments to kids this morning about their thinking emphasized that,' agreed Judy. 'If you want to follow through from this, where do you see it heading?'

'I think it might be useful to take it a step further — I read an idea some time ago for developing an explicit chart of thinking skills. I'll see if I can find it again, and start it off with the kids. Maybe you'd like to add to it when you come in on Monday.'

'I would,' said Judy. 'It helps kids see coherence between what we do, which is a real challenge when we're mostly teaching on different days! I was just wondering, Joan,' Judy concluded, 'If you could give me some quick feedback on the way we've been working this through. I've been trying to ask self-evaluative questions rather than offer advice and I just wondered how that was working for you . . .'

Classroom leaders:
▼ Help colleagues to reflect and self-evaluate
▼ Seek feedback
▼ Use a metacognitive approach to their own learning
▼ Understand the power of peer coaching

▼ *DEMONSTRATING LEADERSHIP SKILLS* ▼

The leadership at Mansfield Park Primary School is shared and enhanced in a myriad of ways by staff, and principal, Toni Cocchiaro. Staff meetings are run by staff, all contribute to the agenda and daily bulletin, teachers chair the many and various committees within the school, and all contribute to policy development and decision making. This collaborative staff lead workshops both within the school and across the state, and organize open days by request for interested teachers to visit and observe their programs in practice.

Such is their commitment to learning partnerships that they include and involve the parent community wherever possible.

And such is their modelling of effective leadership that students are able to develop their own leadership skills, an example of which is seen here:

T-BALL LUNCHTIME ACTIVITY

The Junior Primary children can play T-Ball and practise catching and throwing to each other. It will happen Wednesday lunchtime on the oval and Thursday lunchtime in the JP yard. Could you please pass this on to your children. Thanks.

Christine and Lisa Room 12

Extract from the school daily bulletin

In addition to well-known structures such as student representatives council, cross-age peer tutoring and running their own class meetings, students broadcast announcements, use bulletin display boards, contribute to the school's daily bulletin, organize lunch-time activities, manage their own sports organization, train younger children as traffic monitors, speak at staff meetings, undertake surveys and the occasional petition, and provide positive and specific support towards the integration of children with special needs.

When teachers actively work at developing their own leadership skills, everyone around them grows!

Classroom leaders:
▼ Demonstrate leadership skills

▼ *NETWORKING* ▼

Teaching and living are both complex undertakings these days. The teachers we know who lead balanced lives and make a difference in the lives of the children they teach understand the importance of developing personal and professional networks.

They commit time and energy to developing and maintaining these sometimes fragile networks, constantly monitoring to ensure balance between the two.

The metaphor of the open hands is indicative of the support and strength needed from and provided by an effective network.

Personal network   Professional newtwork

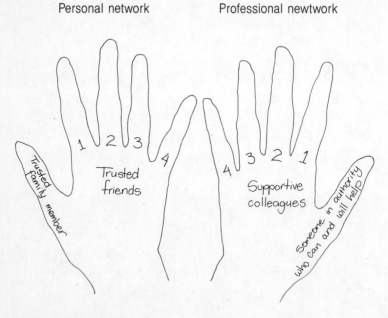

Classroom leaders:
▼ Develop effective networks

▼ ASKING HARD QUESTIONS ▼

Joan's Journal   November 18

I had a lovely surprise today in a letter from Martin
C. whom I taught in a multi-age class back in 1974.
He's almost finished his teaching degree and tracked
me down through 'Adventures in Thinking.'
It brought all sorts of memories back - the 'Circus
McGurkus' the kids organised and ran for parents, the
day I left Jane asleep in the sickbay the sight of
Lance with big boots, no socks on (as usual), and grime
an inch thick, grinning as he gave me a bunch of pink
carnations at Christmas. And I certainly remember
the struggle I had with Mr. S. about the dratted graded
reading series used in the school. I can hear his words
even now: "You can't let Martin go past 'dark green' level.
What will he read next year?" In those days, junior staff
members did what they were told by senior staff-as a
student and a teacher I had never been encouraged
to question or challenge authority - it just wasn't done.
However the thought of Martin becoming frustrated and
losing the joy he found in reading somehow gave me
the courage to question his assumptions and talk things
through with Mr. S. He really listened, and it turned out
that he had no educational justification for his view at all,
(which I would know now, but didn't then!) and admitted it.
In fact, it led to a major discussion at a staff meeting, and
the way in which readers were used was completely
turned around — a big move in those days!

Classroom leaders:
▼ Have the courage to question

▼ UNDERSTANDING YOUR PURPOSE ▼

Joan's Journal   March 15

I remember very clearly my first year of teaching at East
Brunswick Primary School. It seemed as if I lived there at
weekends as well, painting chairs and tables, making chair-bags,
finding resources and creating exciting learning challenges. I had
38 preps, many of whom had just arrived from Greece or Italy.
I truly loved teaching and it always seemed somewhat of a
surprise to get a salary cheque every second Thursday for
something I loved doing so much. After three years, some of
my friends asked whether I'd ever get promoted beyond prep!
What funny conceptions non-teachers can have about the
teaching profession!

As I reflect back over my teaching years, I know that I've
been fortunate enough to experience many different roles
in education. When I was first appointed as a district
consultant, I'd been teaching for about thirteen years. I remember
feeling delighted with my new title - educational consultant.
How grand it sounded, and how much grander each new title
sounded as the years went by - deputy principal, author,
curriculum officer, senior education officer, lecturer....

But what these roles and associated experiences have actually helped me learn is self-awareness, greater inner confidence, and a clearer sense of purpose. Even my recent experience of working by invitation with business and industry has helped me understand the difference between what I *can* do and what I *choose* to do. And my choice is teaching - whether it be with kids or adults.

Sometimes when I am working with teachers, I'll hear one of them share what they do by saying "I'm just a classroom teacher". What I've learned is that there is no more important job than teaching. And now that I'm older (and hopefully wiser) I know that grand titles are just external labels and that true teachers teach from within. Now, when people ask me what I do, I am proud to say "I teach."

Classroom leaders:
▼ Consciously recommit to teaching

Thinking and reflecting on our learning and teaching, having the opportunity to work in many classrooms and in a range of collegial ways with teachers, and working through the process and unfolding of this book, has had a powerful impact on our own self-growth. Not only have we gained deepened insights into ourselves, our beliefs, our teaching, our principles and purposes, but we have had reinforced for us time and time again that principle-centred teaching is a life-long quest. It requires commitment to continual learning and hard work — but, oh, what a joyful adventure it can be!

To work on self-growth

▼ Work on knowing self
▼ Constantly seek to make links in learning
▼ Affirm yourself
▼ Reflect on your learning
▼ Integrate personal and professional growth
▼ Seek balance in your life
▼ Show passion for learning and teaching
▼ Be assertive
▼ Acknowledge your mistakes
▼ Give and accept peer support
▼ Consciously set out to learn from others
▼ Commit to working with colleagues
▼ Understand key leadership skills
▼ Constantly seek to improve your learning and teaching
▼ Take risks in your own learning
▼ Help colleagues to reflect and self-evaluate
▼ Seek feedback
▼ Use a metacognitive approach to your own learning
▼ Understand the power of peer coaching
▼ Demonstrate leadership skills
▼ Develop effective networks
▼ Have the courage to question
▼ Consciously recommit to teaching

Reflecting on self-growth

'In order to improve others one must first improve oneself.'

For me this quote means:

I believe I already implement the following principles from this section:

Feedback from my learning partner/friend/colleague tells me I am good at:

One aspect of myself I would like to work on is:

Ways in which I will become more effective at this include:

I plan to monitor my progress and seek feedback in the following ways:

Notes and thoughts

On reflection

Remember that the oak tree
grows so tall and strong
because it grows slowly and well.

A Discussion

Reflection is both an integral and an essential component of the learning process. Learning needs to be constant, lifelong and dynamic, and helping young people to develop a love of learning, an understanding of their own processes, and an acceptance of responsibility for self and others through reflection and self-evaluation is the process and gift of education for which we, as teachers, are responsible.

To help children understand the purpose and value of reflection in their own learning we need to create and take time ourselves to reflect on such things as our personal learning processes, our mode of operation, our philosophy of education, our attitudes toward our students, our peers, and our profession. Through doing this we build a solid foundation for the continuing development and evolution of our own personal and professional lives, and ultimately it influences the lives of our students in more positive and meaningful ways.

This book evolved through a process of extensive reflection about the learning we have gained from our interactions with highly professional teachers, committed to their own learning, their profession, and their students, and throughout the book we have tried to model a range of different strategies and processes. In providing both a brief structured reflection and an open space for your personal thoughts, feelings, jottings and learnings at the end of each section, we have deliberately aimed to cater for different preferences by modelling just some of the broad spectrum of reflective and self-evaluative strategies we need to experience ourselves as teachers in order to help our students.

We hope that you'll think of a range of ways to make use of this book for your own personal reflection, as a means of raising issues for discussion and further exploration with colleagues, perhaps even as a resource to help your school community to clarify a shared set of beliefs and principles by which it operates.

This final section is designed to help *you* to:
- acknowledge learning as a dynamic process which needs to be approached in personally appropriate and manageable ways
- reflect on and evaluate your personal integration of the principles outlined in the book
- develop a 'picture' of your professional strengths and challenges.

The information in this section may be used in a number of different ways. Some suggestions are:
- following the process outlined in methods 1 or 2
- using the issues raised for you as the basis for discussion in a peer coaching session
- with a trusted colleague, agree to using methods 1 *or* 2 as outlined. First, develop wheels for yourselves, then do one for each other, based on the picture you have of that person. Compare the two wheels you now each have, using them as the basis for feedback, discussion, and planning.
- integrating these principles as part of a more formal evaluation and planning process
- using the information in your own highly creative way and choosing to provide us with some feedback!

When you have completed your preferred method, study the shape and balance of the wheel. How smoothly would it roll? What are your strengths? Which sections do you feel really confident about? Which sections do you need to work on? How many points were you able to plot on the outer rims of the wheel? (How many 4s and 5s did you give yourself?)

Which are the principles you scored yourself low on? Which were the lowest? How will you plan to maintain the things you are strong in? What and who will help you to work on the areas that need building? Which is the first area you would like to work on? What will that look like when you are doing it really well? What are the first steps you need to take for this?

The self-contract on pages 133-4 is included to help you to clarify some goals and future directions and provides one way to make a written commitment to your own learning, teaching and leadership growth.

A Process

Read through each individual principle on pages 128 to 132 and assign yourself a number for that principle using the following code:
1 = I achieve this rarely
2 = I manage this sometimes
3 = I do this often
4 = I am happy with my ability to do this most of the time
5 = I am highly competent in achieving this

Using method 1

Map your score for each seperate principle on the wheel. (There is a separate line to correspond to the number of principles in each section.)

Join together each of your marks.

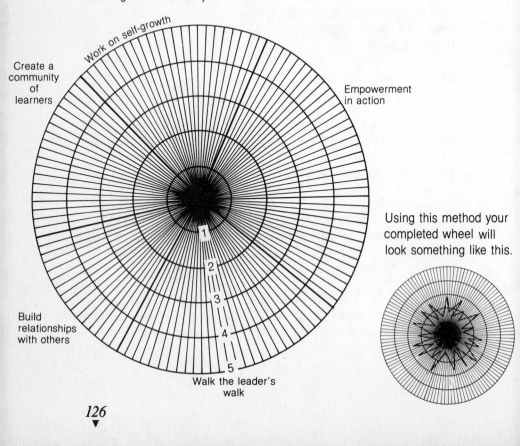

Work on self-growth

Create a
community
of
learners

Empowerment
in action

Using this method your
completed wheel will
look something like this.

Build
relationships
with others

1
2
3
4
5

Walk the leader's
walk

Using method 2

At the end of each section TOTAL YOUR SCORE and determine an average for that section.

Mark the averages on the wheel.

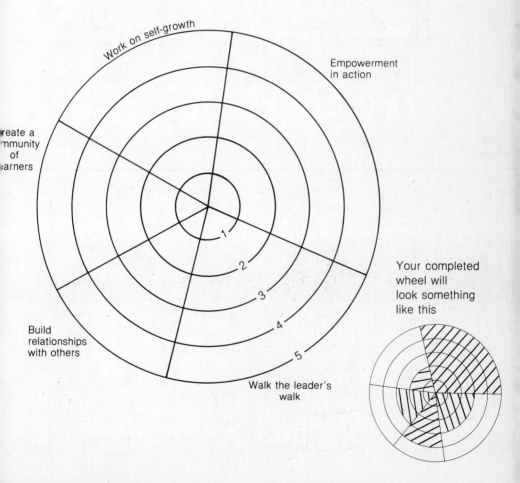

Work on self-growth

Empowerment
in action

Create a
community
of
learners

Build
relationships
with others

Walk the leader's
walk

Your completed
wheel will
look something
like this

To empower growth in others

My number between 1-5
for this 'I statement' is:

▼ I provide real think-time	
▼ I promote engagement in authentic, purposeful learning	
▼ I offer open-ended learning opportunities	
▼ I work to make learning enjoyable	
▼ I build on from what learners know and can do	
▼ I explain purposes clearly	
▼ I make use of visual organizers	
▼ I encourage thinking in metaphor	
▼ I take time to support individuals	
▼ I give feedback on observations	
▼ I help realistic goal-setting	
▼ I encourage learners to ask their own questions and seek their own answers	
▼ I am prepared to share my power to empower my students	
▼ I use a variety of teaching strategies	
▼ I foster learning with and from peers	
▼ I work to develop understandings of many ways of learning	
▼ I apreciate the importance of imagination in learning	
▼ I help learners to use the metacognitive cycle of plan-monitor-evaluate	
▼ I help learners to develop context appropriate strategies	
▼ I encourage risk-taking in learning	
▼ I focus on learner self-evaluation	
▼ I work to develop learner responsibility to self and others	
▼ I reframe mistake-making	
▼ I invite responsible choice-making	
▼ I model using self-talk	
▼ Include the use of multi-modal strategies	
▼ I capitalize on opportunities presented by conflict	
▼ I develop mutually high expectations	
▼ I share leadership and responsibility	
▼ I engage learners in on-going reflection	

Continued

▼ I encourage personal connection-making	
▼ I give meaningful praise	
▼ I involve learners in their own assessment	
▼ I foster learning transfer to other situations	
▼ I model my own reflection and learning	
TOTAL	
÷ 35 average =	

To walk the leader's walk

▼ I acknowledge the complexity of my role	
▼ I clarify roles and expectations	
▼ I am clear about what I value	
▼ I am able to develop a shared vision for what learning and education can be	
▼ I introduce learners to role models	
▼ I believe in learners and help learners to believe in themselves	
▼ I make explicit the skills needed for success	
▼ I am organized	
▼ I am able to think big and start small	
▼ I work on what I can influence	
▼ I think and act win-win	
▼ I choose to think, act and speak positively	
▼ I have a positive orientation toward change	
▼ I trust my intuition	
▼ I co-create knowledge with other learners	
▼ I understand the importance of humour	
▼ I use humour appropriately	
▼ I integrate rather than add concepts and ideas	
▼ I try to walk the walk rather than talk the talk	

Continued

▼ I follow through and keep commitments	
▼ I use the teachable moments	
▼ I am both flexible and consistent	
▼ I work to develop a global view	
▼ I am committed to a professional code of ethics	
▼ I display integrity and personal dignity	
▼ I make a leadership contribution beyond the classroom	
▼ I am aware of my leadership skills and am proud to be a teacher	
TOTAL	
÷ 27 average =	

To build relationships with others

▼ I aim to listen more and talk less	
▼ I talk with people rather than at them	
▼ I am conscious of noticing and acknowledging others' feelings	
▼ I acknowledge many aspects of people's lives	
▼ I remember to attend to the little things as well as the big ones	
▼ I give congruent messages	
▼ I understand the power of non-verbal messages	
▼ I am prepared to share something of myself with others	
▼ I invite others' ideas and act on them	
▼ I demonstrate trust	
▼ I understand and seek to accommodate people's basic needs	
▼ I promote empathy for others' viewpoints	
▼ I explicitly develop social skills	
▼ I am patient	
▼ I care enough to confront constructively	
▼ I am consistent in the way I treat people	
TOTAL	
÷ 16 average =	

To create a community of learners

▼ I build a class team	
▼ I ensure that each person has a part to play	
▼ I work to create a stimulating classroom environment	
▼ I have a 'circle' philosphy	
▼ I make explicit what is valued	
▼ I aim to build a common language	
▼ I spend time developing consistent procedures	
▼ I engage learners in evaluating aspects of classroom life	
▼ I invite shared decision-making	
▼ I provide for many modes of learning	
▼ I encourage the use of learners' strengths	
▼ I include and challenge all learners	
▼ I show that I value difference	
▼ I balance individual and team learning	
▼ I balance the way learning teams are formed	
▼ I develop genuine partnerships with parents	
▼ I model inclusive language	
▼ I celebrate individual and class successes	
▼ I appreciate and utilize the rich learning resources of the community	
TOTAL	
÷ 19 average =	

To work on self-growth

▼ I work on knowing myself	
▼ I constantly seek to make links In learning	
▼ I am able to affirm myself	
▼ I constantly reflect on my own learning	
▼ I seek to integrate my personal and professional growth	
▼ I seek balance in my life	
▼ I am passionate about learning and teaching	

Continued

▼ I am assertive	
▼ I am prepared to acknowledge my mistakes	
▼ I give and accept peer support	
▼ I consciously set out to learn from others	
▼ I commit to working with colleagues	
▼ I understand key leadership skills	
▼ I constantly seek to improve my learning and teaching	
▼ I take risks in my own learning	
▼ I help colleagues to reflect and self-evaluate	
▼ I seek feedback	
▼ I use a metacognitive approach to my own learning	
▼ I understand and use the power of peer coaching	
▼ I demonstrate my leadership skills	
▼ I develop effective networks	
▼ I have the courage to question	
▼ I consciously recommit to teaching	
TOTAL	
÷ 23 average =	

A self-contract

I feel reassured that I do have the following strengths:

Something significant I have learned from this book has been:

Specific challenges I plan to set as personal goals for myself are:
For this term   For this year   Over three years

I will need the following resources and support to achieve my goals:

I will begin to gather this support by:

I plan to monitor my progress by:

I will have satisfied myself that I have achieved my goal(s) when:

I plan to celebrate by:

A final thought

As a final thought, we would like to share with you a piece of philosophy which is integral to our beliefs about inspiring classroom leadership:

*When you give away
some of the light from a candle
by lighting another person's flame
there isn't any less light
because you've given some away
there's more.
When everybody grows,
there isn't less of anybody
there's more of
and for — everybody.*

Kaleel Jamison

Recommended reading

Bellanca, J., Fogarty, R. & Dalton, J. *Blueprints for Thinking in the Co-operative Classroom,* Australian Edition, Hawker Brownlow, Melbourne, 1992.

Caine, R. & Caine, G. *Making Connections: Teaching and the Human Brain,* available from ASCD, 1250 N. Pitt Street, Alexandria, VA 22314-1403, USA.

Collis, M. & Dalton, J. *Becoming Responsible Learners: Strategies for Positive Classroom Management.* Eleanor Curtain, Melbourne, 1990.

Covey, S. *The 7 Habits of Highly Effective People.* Simon & Schuster, New York, 1989.

Dalton, J. *Adventures in Thinking,* Nelson, Melbourne, 1985.

Dalton, J. & Smith, D. *Extending Childrens Special Abilities,* Ministry of Education, Victoria.

Graves, N. & Graves T. (Ed) Lacey K. *A Part to Play: Tips, Techniques and Tools for Learning Co-operatively,* Latitude Publications, Melbourne, 1990.

Ferguson, M. *The Aquarian Conspiracy,* Palladin, London, 1980.

Fischer & Ury *Getting to Yes,* Arrow Books, London, 1987.

Gardner, H. *The Unschooled Mind: How Children Think and How Schools Should Teach,* Basic Books, USA, 1991.

Glasser, W. *Control Theory in the Classroom,* Harper and Row, New York, 1986.

Hill, S. & Hill, T. *The Collaborative Classroom: A Guide to Co-operative Learning,* Eleanor Curtain, Melbourne, 1990.

Houston, J. *The Possible Human,* St Martins Press, Los Angeles, 1982.

Johnson, D. & Johnson, R. *Leading the Co-operative School,* Interaction Book Co, Minnesota, 1989.

McCabe, M. & Rhoades, J. *The Nurturing Classroom,* ITA Publications, 1989 (available in Australia through Teamlinks Australia)

Myers, N. *The GAIA Atlas of Future Worlds: Challenge and Opportunity in an Age of Change,* Penguin, London, 1990.

Naisbitt, J. & Aburdene, P. *Megatrends 2000,* Pan Books, 1990.

Peck, M. Scott *The Different Drum,* Simon & Schuster, New York, 1987.

Reid, J., Forrestal, P. & Cook, J. *Small Group Learning in the Classroom,* Chalkface Press, Perth, 1989.

Roddick, A. *Body and Soul,* Ebury Press, 1991.

Rogers, W. *You Know the Fair Rule,* Australian Council for Educational Research, Melbourne, 1990.

Samples, B. *Open Mind, Whole Mind,* Jalmar Press, Rolling Hills Estates, California, 1987.

Ornstein, R. & Erlich, P. *New World, New Mind: Changing the Way We Think to Save Our Future,* Palladin, London, 1991.

Acknowledgements

For their stories and/or photographs we thank the following individuals:

Glenn Bromfield	Annette Salter
Roger Edmunds	Warren Pill
Jill Davis	Denise Armstrong
Faye Blackhurst	Sue Ryan
Mary-Ann Griggs	Neil Bolton
Fiona Jarvis	Christopher Nichols
Narelle Kidson	Tony Ryan
Di Tait	Carole Cooper
Judy Stevens	Joan Kreemers
Geraldine Peters	Paul Carmody
Miranda Armstrong	

The cartoon on p. 11 is reproduced with permission of the Tasmanian Department of Education and the Arts.

We acknowledge that contributions were drawn from real classrooms in the following schools:
Campbelltown District High School — Tasmania
Upper Burnie Primary School — Tasmania
Montague Bay Primary School — Tasmania
Taperoo Primary School — South Australia
Perth Primary School — Tasmania
Orford Primary School — Tasmania
Hale School — Western Australia
Penguin Primary School — Tasmania
Mansfield Park Primary School — South Australia
Eltham College — Victoria

We thank all teachers who provided the bases for the illustrations used in 'I Teach', and we thank our families for their love and their continuing support for our work.